Contents

12/10/95

GW00566553

Introduction

This book offers practical suggestions to teachers faced with organising group craft sessions, in the hope that, being well prepared, both teacher and students will have the maximum opportunity of enjoying the creativity which craftwork affords.

The book is not intended solely for use in schools, but is designed to be of assistance to any leader, whether part of a youth organisation, Cub/Scout/Guide company or other leisure group. There are many volunteer groups whose leaders find themselves having to organise sessions of craft but do not realise that a successful session depends very much on the preparation. Some may be apprehensive of approaching such a task. Even teachers in schools who have some experience of this practical work are always looking for new ideas.

It is also hoped that much contained within the following pages will fire the enthusiasm of individuals who enjoy craftwork and who will find suggestions relevant to their own hobby.

To the organiser

The book contains nineteen chapters, each one dealing with a different item of craftwork. There is a wide variety of media to use and most of the materials are easily obtainable.

Each chapter is set out in three parts:

1. Step-by-step instructions with diagrams;

2. Suggestions and hints for preparing the materials – together with a diagram of the work area which can be used as a 'check-list' to ensure that all the necessary materials have been provided;

3. Full-size patterns for copying.

Try it out first

Although it is hoped that all the pitfalls have been identified in each chapter, teachers and leaders are strongly advised to work through the chosen craft to produce a finished example before attempting it with a group of students. This has two advantages. The students will be more highly motivated to produce the work if they can see, handle and examine a completed example before they commence work. Many will be able to see ways in which they can adapt the basic design to reflect their own individuality. By working through the instructions and producing a sample of the work, the teacher will gain first-hand experience of the materials and method and be better prepared to help students overcome any section where difficulties may be encountered.

Use as a reference book

The book contains many helpful suggestions for using raw materials: for example mixing paint, conserving card, preparing a glaze. It is hoped that readers will find that the book becomes a useful addition either to the school library or to their own personal bookshelves.

Adapt the materials

Materials for the items of craft have been recommended because of their suitability for the work. However, as new products come on to the market and existing materials improve, a wider variety will, doubtless, be available to choose from. Experiment and adapt the materials to suit the circumstances.

Develop the ideas

Many of the ideas included in the book give only an introduction to a particular craft. It may be that, after successfully completing the initial item, students or individuals will be enthusiastic to develop the idea and produce their own unique piece of work. On the other hand, if any item is considered too difficult for a particular age range, there is scope for the teacher to scale down the degree of difficulty by replacing the item with something more simple whilst still using the basic techniques of the medium.

Use the patterns

All the patterns required for a particular piece of work have been reproduced, full size, at the end of the relevant chapter. These may be traced or photocopied and templates or sheets of patterns made for the students' use. Again, these patterns may be adapted to any requirements and are useful to have to hand for reference.

Make up the charts

More than one craft can be offered during a session with the help of the simplified craft charts to be found at the end of the book. These are included so that teachers can make up their own, full-size, versions for display in the work area. After the teacher has given a brief introduction to each craft on offer, students can choose the item they wish to make and, with the materials prepared and available, begin immediately. Should the teacher be engaged with one group, other students can progress with their own craft by following the displayed chart until help is available.

Finally, trying to organise and complete any task with a a group of youngsters is a totally different experience from sitting quietly at home and working at a craft. Craftwork is one of the most exacting practical activities to organise with any group. There is certainly an art in it. It is hoped that these pages will assist in overcoming some of the more common pitfalls and heartaches and it is to this end that the experiences of success and failure are shared here.

| Stone Painting

Painted stones can be used as paper-weights or door stops depending on their size. They are colourful and unusual gifts.

METHOD

1. Using the pencil, draw a line around the stone just below half way. You will be painting the surface down to this line.

2. Draw your design on the stone. If you keep the pattern or picture bold, the areas of colour will be easier to fill with paint.

3. Paint each area. Remember that the background colour goes down to the pencil line.

Clean the brush carefully between colours.

4. When it is dry, use a thin brush and black paint and go over each of the lines you drew in pencil, to outline your picture. This will separate the colours and 'bring them to life'.

5. While the paint is drying, cut out a shape from felt which is large enough to cover the part of the base which comes into contact with the table.

6. Stick the felt to the underside of the stone, pressing it down firmly, especially round the edges.

7. Varnish all the paintwork, right down to the original line. Leave to dry.

   Clean the varnish brush in the white spirit.

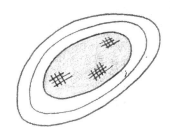

ORGANISING YOUR MATERIALS

I. Setting up the work area

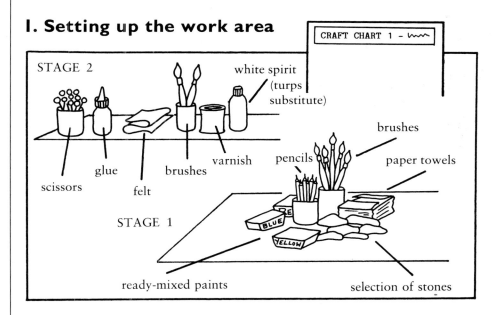

(a) Set up the table(s) with enough equipment to enable each child to begin work immediately.

(b) Ensure that all children have adequate working space.

2. Brushes

Store brushes either flat or standing on their handles. Never allow children to stand brushes on the bristles for long periods. This will ruin the brushes. Use a solid container which will not tip over when brushes are removed. Alternatively, place a stone in the bottom of the container for extra ballast.

3. Water pots

Use water pots which will not spill easily. They should be filled no more than half full and children should be encouraged to change the water frequently to keep brushes and paint clean. Alternately, provide a sufficient number of brushes so that each one can be left in a particular colour for the duration of the session, thus making the use of water pots unnecessary.

4. Paint

When organising paint for use by children, use a water-based paint which can be removed easily from clothing, hands and hair!

Prepare powder or ready-mixed paint by mixing a quantity of each colour with a small amount of PVA adhesive medium. This is ideal for stone painting as it thickens the colours, speeds up drying and leaves the stone with a slightly glazed finish so that the paint does not rub off with handling.

If paint is kept in clean margarine tubs with lids, it can be 'topped-up' occasionally and kept for long periods. Mark each lid with the colour contained in the tub (it saves time searching for the one you want!).

For older children and adults, enamel paints can be used. These give the same, glossy effect without the need for varnish but do require more care during use to keep clean and prevent spillage. Use white spirit to clean the brushes.

5. Keeping work area clean

Most work surfaces will either be made from a wipe-clean material or covered with a plastic cloth or newspaper before the equipment is set out. However, it is useful to have a number of paper towels handy for use during the session. The children can use these to stand their stones on during painting and this also helps in moving the stone when completed. Paper towels are also useful for wiping brushes and cleaning up any accidental spillages.

6. Selection of stones

Unless the children are supplying their own stones, time must be spent in selecting suitable stones for painting. Light-coloured stones are preferable, as pencil lines will show up easily. A selection should be available on the table at the start of the session. Some children may work quickly and get through two or three in a session, so make sure you have enough. It is also possible to recycle any stones which are 'mistakes' by soaking them in water and using a scrubbing brush to remove the existing paintwork. These can be left to dry and included in the next session.

7. Finishing touches

Although it is suggested that felt is used for the base pad, any material will do the job. The same type of PVA glue which was used in mixing the paint is ideal for sticking the base to the stone. Ensure that enough glue is placed at the edge of the material shape so that no fraying is possible.

It is also suggested that the stone is varnished to give it a completely finished look. This stage may be omitted but does make the piece of work look better, especially if it is to be a gift. Use a polyurethane varnish and a large paintbrush. When the paintwork on the stone is completely dry, start at the underside of the stone where the original line was drawn, and paint the varnish over the design, with long, gentle strokes. Do not allow children to 'stir up' the varnish as this causes bubbles and spoils the finished effect. Complete by standing the stone on its base and working from one side to the other with smooth strokes. Some absorbent surfaces may require two coasts of varnish. Apply the second coat when the first coat has dried.

Clean the brush thoroughly with white spirit. If a number of children are to use the varnish, the brushes may be left in white spirit until the end of the session.

DESIGNS FOR STONE PAINTING

Copy the design directly on to the stone or trace the picture and transfer it to the stone using carbon paper.

9

2 Finger Puppets

Use this basic idea to create your own space monster, cartoon favourites or a character from a pantomime, nativity play or folk tale.

METHOD

1. Trace the template of the head and body from those at the end of this chapter and transfer them to thick card using carbon paper.

Fold tracing paper around the card

Insert the carbon paper

2. Colour the head and body with felt pens.

3. Go over all the details with a black felt pen to outline them. Cut out the head and body.

4. Put a small dab of glue at the top of the neck and stick the head in position. You can create character by placing the head at an angle.

5. Bend the puppet's shoes forward so that it stands on the table.

6. From the thin card, cut two rectangles. Roll one into a tube which will fit your index finger. Glue it. Roll the second rectangle into a tube which will fit your middle finger. Glue it.

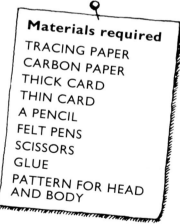

7. When the tubes are dry, glue them to the backs of the puppet's legs, at knee level.

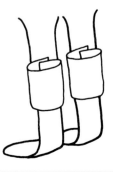

Materials required
TRACING PAPER
CARBON PAPER
THICK CARD
THIN CARD
A PENCIL
FELT PENS
SCISSORS
GLUE
PATTERN FOR HEAD AND BODY

ORGANISING YOUR MATERIALS

1. Setting up the work area

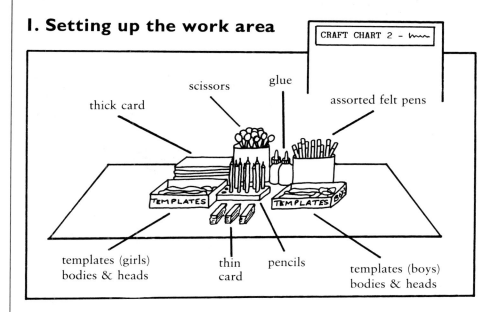

CRAFT CHART 2 -

thick card

scissors

glue

assorted felt pens

TEMPLATES

TEMPLATES

templates (girls)
bodies & heads

thin
card

pencils

templates (boys)
bodies & heads

When working with a group of children (however small the group may be) difficulties will arise if they are expected to trace the patterns and use the carbon paper. Therefore it is well worth spending extra time in preparation.

2. Templates

Using the method of copying with carbon paper, prepare a few templates from card which the children can use to draw round. Only the outlines need be traced as children will enjoy creating the puppet's clothing and facial features. If you give them too many details, all the puppets will look exactly alike and there will be no scope for individuality.

3. Card

Ensure that the card is thick enough for the puppet to stay upright when being displayed but not so thick that the children have difficulty cutting it.

If the amount of thick card available is limited or expensive, then conserve it either by
(a) marking out the puppets on the card before the session starts
(b) or by cutting the card into 'puppet-sized' pieces for distribution.

Given a free hand on a large sheet of card, children will automatically use the middle of it and waste the rest! Guillotine the thin card into 2.5 cm × 8 cm strips.

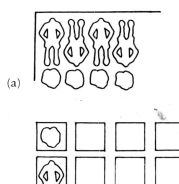

(a)

(b)

4. Colouring

Colouring the puppets before cutting out is by far the most simple method. Encourage the children to outline *all* the colours as this will bring the puppet's colours out and make them more definite. Trying to outline *after* cutting is a very tedious job.

5. Cutting the arms

Young children will find the process of cutting out the space inside the arms an impossible task. Either leave the card there or cut it for them, using a sharp craft knife and resting on thick cardboard to protect the work surface.

Older children will manage this task if shown how to begin with a star in the centre of the space, then working outwards with the scissors.

6. Tubes

The puppets are worked by inserting the index and middle fingers into the tubes, from above. As index and middle fingers are usually of differing sizes, ensure that each child attaches the correct size of tube to each leg.

TEMPLATES FOR FINGER PUPPETS

13

3 Quilling

Quilling is an old craft now enjoying a revival. Originally done on quills (hence the name) it is the craft of rolling paper – a very therapeutic pastime – and making shapes which fit together to form a picture or design.

METHOD

Start by rolling the end of the paper tightly around the cocktail stick. You may prefer to roll the rest of the strip in your fingers as you can then keep the sides of the paper in line.

Shapes to make

1. Tight roll

Having rolled the paper into a solid tube, glue the end and press it in place so that it remains in a solid coil.

2. Loose roll

Roll the strip of paper into a tight roll. Hold the end of the strip in one hand and draw the cocktail stick back through the roll so that it pulls open. Place the roll on the table and glue the end in place.

3. Tear drop

Roll the strip into a tight roll. Draw the cocktail stick through the length of the roll to open it and glue the end into position. Using thumb and finger, gently pinch the top layers of the coil to form a peak.

4. Leaf

Roll the strip into a tight roll. Pull the cocktail stick through the length of the coil to open it and glue the end into position. Using thumb and finger, gently pinch the layers at one side to form a peak. Turn the shape round and pinch the opposite side to match.

5. Double roll

Begin at one end, rolling inwards to the centre. Roll the opposite end inwards to meet at the middle. Glue the two rolls so that they hold together. You can keep the rolls tight, or loosen them by pulling the cocktail stick through each one before gluing, or make them of different sizes.

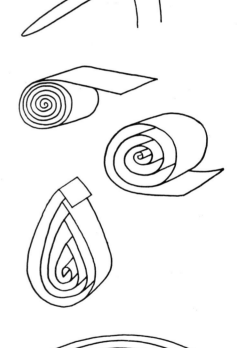

6. Scroll

Roll one end of the strip to the centre; roll the other end the opposite way. The scroll may be glued to keep it tight or opened by drawing the cocktail stick through the coils and then glued at any point along the centre stem. It can even be left completely open.

7. Heart

Fold the strip of paper in half. Roll one end inwards to the centre crease. Roll the other end inwards to match. Open the rolls by drawing the cocktail stick through the coils. Glue the rolls where they touch to keep them in place.

8. Beak

Fold the strip of paper in half. Roll each end *outwards* as far to centre as required. This shape may be glued at the point marked to keep it together or left unglued if a more open shape is needed.

Combining shapes

Insert a tight coil of a different colour into the centre of any of the above shapes. For example, use the leaf with a tight coil in the middle to make an eye. Small coils can be made by using shorter or narrower strips of paper.

Finishing off

Once you have practised these shapes and, perhaps, experimented with some of your own, make up a design for a picture or mobile.

Making a picture

1. Make up all the shapes you need for your picture and position them on a piece of background card.

2. Take one shape at a time and put a tiny drop of glue on the underside of the coils. Gently press into place.

   NB: Some shapes may not lie exactly as you want them to, so use the cocktail stick to even the spacing between the strands. Hold them in place with a finger until the glue has taken (usually just a few seconds).

3. When it is complete, the picture could be mounted and hung on the wall.

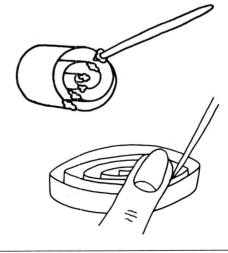

Making a mobile

 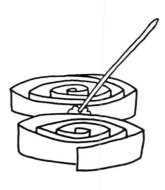 

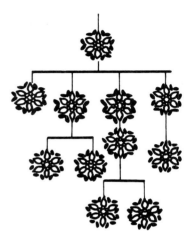

I. Make up all the shapes required for your design and arrange them on the work surface so that the shapes are touching.

2. With a small dab of adhesive, applied with a cocktail stick, glue the shapes together, where they touch. Allow the glue to dry before lifting up the completed design.

3. Attach a piece of cotton or nylon fishing-line to the top point of your work and hang it up.

4. More complicated mobiles may be made using florists' wire for ribs.

ORGANISING YOUR MATERIALS

I. Setting up the work area

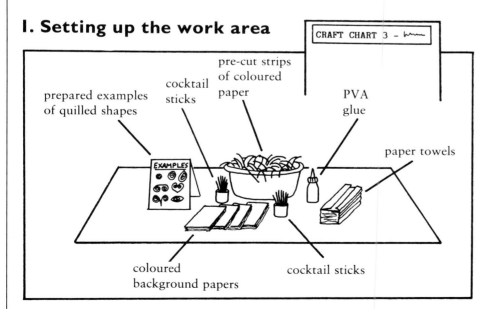

The overall impression of the work area, once it is set out, can be rather uninteresting to children so, if time allows, make up a few examples to show them before the session starts. A small display of the individual shapes, each labelled with its name, will give the students a better idea of what they can produce.

Quilling has become so popular over recent years that prepared packs can be bought from most craft shops and educational suppliers. However, it is unnecessary to spend a lot initially, as the equipment needed is fairly easy to obtain.

2. Paper

(a) Any paper can be used. Even white writing paper, quilled and mounted on a dark background, can look very sophisticated.

(b) Sugar paper is ideal. This stiff matt craft paper can be purchased at most large stationers and comes in a variety of colours. All educational suppliers carry a stock of sugar paper, and many of them supply packets of assorted bright colours (rainbow paper).

(c) Coloured streamers (the kind you throw at New Year's Eve parties) can also be used for quilling but these are very narrow and flimsy and should only be used after experience with more substantial types of paper. Young children will certainly find these difficult to work with.

Prepare the paper in advance of the session. Use either a guillotine (or craft knife and metal rule, resting on a thick piece of cardboard) to cut the strips. Try to keep them as uniform in width as possible as this will affect the height of the finished piece of work.

It is suggested that the strips are cut 1 cm wide as this is quite a good size for children to cope with. The strips can be any length, but about 20 cm is good for a start. Any strip can be shortened if a smaller shape is required.

Place the strips in a container on the work surface so that they are to hand when needed. The container can be 'topped up' as required with any or all of the colours, and these can also be stored in the container for future use.

3. Cocktail sticks

Cocktail sticks (preferably wooden ones as these have no moulded ridges running down their lengths) are available at most stores. Place a few in a small pot on the work surface.

Children will need two each – a 'dry' one for rolling the paper and the other to apply the glue.

4. Glue

Use a PVA adhesive. This white, water-based glue dries completely transparent and, however messy a piece of work may look at completion (within reason, of course), any mess will virtually disappear once the glue has dried.

One pot of glue should be enough for a whole table. Children can squeeze a small blob of glue onto a paper towel and use it from there with a cocktail stick. Only a minute amount is required on each quilled shape, to hold its position.

5. Paper towels (or piece of newspaper)

This is a useful item for each child to have. It gives them a 'territory' on which to store their finished shapes and prevents work 'spreading' and getting lost into someone else's picture.

It also conserves the glue, as each child only needs a small blob of glue at a time, and it protects the work surface from unwanted spillages.

6. Background papers

Cut some multi-coloured rainbow paper into A5 size sheets (15 cm × 21 cm). Children can select the colour they want for their background and mount their designs.

Children could work together in groups to produce a mobile – each child being responsible for one element on the mobile. Or try a class frieze done in quilling, for a change.

Combine shapes to make this peacock.

DESIGNS FOR MOBILES

A simple pattern for a caterpillar.

Try a more complicated floral design.

4 Paper Sculpture

Paper sculpture is the craft of making three-dimensional models based on simple geometrical shapes. Some practice may be required with the basic shapes before attempting this particular model.

Materials required
CARD
PENCIL
SCISSORS
GLUE
BLACK FELT PEN
TEMPLATES
PAPER-CLIPS

METHOD

1. Place the template shapes on to card, draw round them with the pencil and cut them out.

2. Roll the body piece between the hands so that it forms part of a cone and glue where marked. Use a paper-clip at each end to hold it in position while it dries.

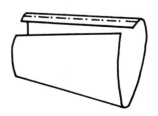

3. Do the same thing with the head piece.

4. Fold the centre pieces of the ears forward and glue these flaps inside the head, one on each side, so that the ears stick out sideways.

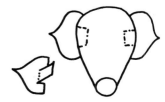

5. Holding the body with the join *upwards* and the head with the join *downwards*, try fitting the two pieces together (without glue for the moment) so that the head sits inside the body at the base of the neck and is level at the forehead. The ears should stick forward from inside the body.

Note where the head touches the body. Glue these places and stick in position.

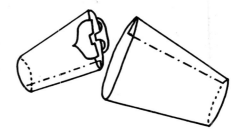

6. Fold the mane in half and fringe both halves with the scissors. Run a line of glue down the centre of the mane and, beginning on the forehead with the wide part of the mane, lay it over the head and as far down the back as it will go.

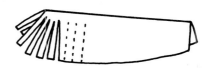

7. Mark the two nostrils on the snout with the felt pen. Run a line of glue around the snout end of the head. Glue the snout in position so that it sticks out all the way round and the barbs are level at each side.

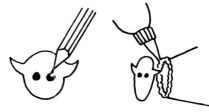

8. Roll the lower part of each tusk around the felt pen (don't forget to make a pair – one left-handed and one right-handed). Glue the tusks half way down the head so that the points slope backwards.

9. Mark the eyes on the head with the felt pen.

10. Roll the four leg pieces around the barrel of the felt tip pen and glue into tubes, where marked.

11. Run a line of glue around the upper, straight edge of the two longer legs and glue these, pointing slightly outwards, as far forward on the body as proportion will allow.

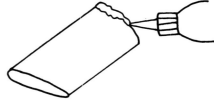

12. Run a line of glue around the top, straight edge of the two shorter legs and glue these, pointing slightly outwards, towards the back of the body so that the model is in proportion and balances.

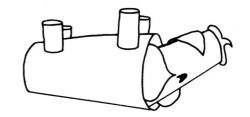

If the model tends to fall forward, adjust the position of the front legs until the right balance is obtained. Lay the hog on his back while the legs dry – they may need support during this stage.

13. Roll the tail piece around the felt pen so that it curls. Glue one end to the inside of the body so that the tail curls upwards.

14. When the model is dry, decorate if required.

ORGANISING YOUR MATERIALS

1. Setting up the work area

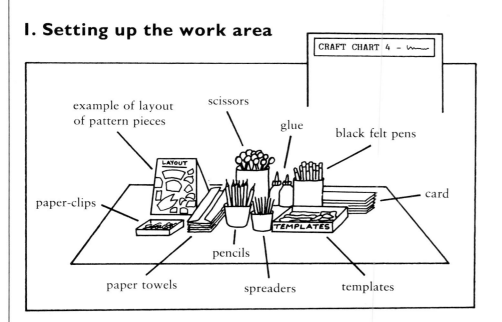

Ensure that all materials are ready for students to begin work immediately as they will need the full session to complete this piece of work.

It is a good idea to have a large box or waste bin available to collect all the offcuts as they occur or the work area will rapidly become a World War III combat zone and vital pieces of the model will disappear.

2. Card

Plain white or slightly tinted manila card is ideal for this type of work. If a thin card is used the model may crumple and if the card is too thick the students will find it difficult to cut and shape.

3. Templates

To conserve the card, there are various ways in which the templates can be organised so that students can still begin work at the same time.

(a) Reproduce the template page at the end of this chapter, either by photocopying or by redrawing onto a master skin. Produce one copy for each student and supply a sheet of card, the same size, onto which the pattern shapes can be redrawn.

(b) Prepare a few sets of templates in strong card and put each shape into a separate pot marked with the name of that piece. i.e. a pot of *heads*, a pot of *bodies*, a pot of *front legs* and so on. Students can then pick the piece required to draw round and put it back in the pot for someone else to use. Each student will need a piece of card on which to draw the pattern and an example of the suggested layout should be available for them to follow – there is one on the craft chart, or the pattern page at the end of this chapter can be made available as a guide.

(c) If your photocopier, Gestetner or Banda will take sheets of manila card, prepare a master with the pattern layout drawn on to it and reproduce a sheet of card, already marked out with the pattern pieces, for each student.

4. Glue

Use a PVA adhesive as this bonds fairly quickly, is easily washed out of clothing and dries transparent. Students should be encouraged to use only *small* amounts of glue on their models to cut down drying time and mess. Provide a cocktail stick or spreader, or even a piece of offcut card, with which to apply the glue. There is no need to provide each student with a pot of glue. A small amount in a paper cup or on a paper towel will be adequate.

Students may find difficulty in gluing card together without the aid of tabs. After applying glue to a rim, the glued edge should be held *downwards* so that the glue remains on the rim and does not run down the length of the shape. If this process proves too difficult, small tabs of offcut card can be made to help join the pieces together.

5. Techniques and danger zones

Keep a careful watch at the following stages to prevent students from doing the wrong thing and becoming despondent:

(a) *Drawing out the shapes* – left to themselves, children will space the pieces out on the card far more than necessary and then complain that the card is not big enough. Encourage them to place each piece so that it is almost touching the previous one, and to follow the layout shown.

(b) *Fringing the mane* – there is bound to be one child who cuts into the fold of the mane instead of fringing the open edge. Point this out to them at the beginning and ensure that they '*hold the fold*' when cutting the mane.

If a curly mane is wanted, cut the fringing and then pull a pair of closed scissors along each fringe from the centre to the edge. Ensure that the card is held and supported firmly or the student may tear the fringe away.

(c) *Rolling the card* – rolling the two large pieces in the hands, before gluing, helps to shape the card so that no creases occur. This rolling should be done very gently so that the card is *encouraged* into shape rather than folded.

Rolling the leg pieces around the barrel of a felt pen also ensures that there are no straight creases along the length. Do not use a felt pen with a hexagonal or fluted barrel!!

(d) *Balancing the model* – by its very shape, the model is front-heavy. Therefore, it is important to position the legs to counterbalance without making the hog look out of proportion. Keep the front legs as far forward as possible – the bases of the legs are shaped so that they will splay outwards – and note that the back legs will be much further forward than a real hog's legs would be. The actual positioning is not too important as long as the overall effect is pleasing and acceptable.

Should the hog absolutely refuse to keep his chin off the ground, weight his rear end by sticking a thick piece of card or some Blu-Tack under the tail joint – or even insert a paper-clip at the back to give him ballast.

Note:

This particular model is very difficult for *young* children and it is not recommended that they start with something so ambitious. Although most paper sculpture is based on geometrical shapes, it is a craft which lends itself to all ranges of ability and experience. The following pages contain suggestions for paper sculpture which can be used with younger children to give them some experience of modelling with card.

Many of the modern maths schemes now used in primary schools lay stress on the ability to recognise and build geometrical solids. Pupils are also encouraged to become conversant with the nets (plans) which will make up into the various shapes, from the humble cylinder to the complicated stylated-dodecahedron.

These geometrical shapes can form the basis of three-dimensional paper sculpture, and a teacher wishing to integrate the practical art/craft period with this mathematics theme will find that much can be learned by building these solid shapes for a practical purpose.

Accuracy in measurement and folding is vitally important as any fractional error at the start will be magnified as the work progresses and shapes will not fit together properly. Pupils will soon learn this and will be encouraged to work as accurately and neatly as they possibly can.

The following shapes may be practised as individual exercises and then combined to form a three-dimensional abstract or model.

Open-ended cylinder

This is perhaps the most simple shape and a good one with which to start. Use card thick enough to hold its shape but not too thick for pupils to work. Cut out the net and roll it gradually in the hands to encourage it into shape. Use a small amount of glue on the area marked and overlap the ends to form the cylinder. A paper-clip at the top and at the bottom may be used to support the join while it dries.

NB: Encourage pupils to use only as much glue as is really necessary. Too much glue will create a messy piece of work and take a long time to dry.

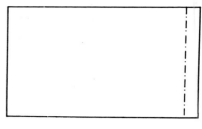

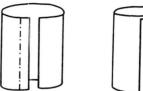

Solid cylinder

Progress to this more advanced shape by affixing solid faces to either or both ends of the cylinder. Circles for either end may be drawn all-in-one with the basic net or cut separately. Ensure that tabs are cut to either the cylinder or the circle for ease of joining.

Remember that length *A* must equal the perimeter of the top circle, plus a small overlap.

An elliptical cylinder may be made in the same way.

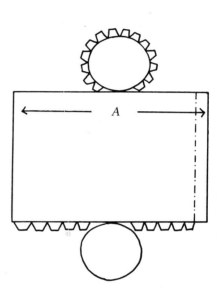

Cube

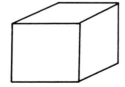

All the sides of a cube are the same length. Follow the shape of the net and ensure that the tabs are large enough to stick comfortably, but taper the tabs to at least 45 degrees to avoid 'bulging' at the corners. There should be seven tabs.

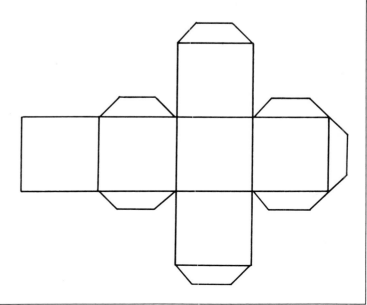

Cuboid

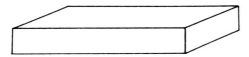

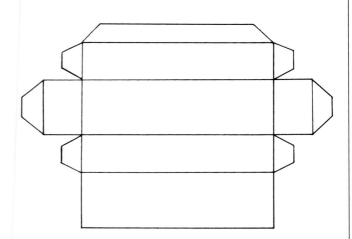

The net uses three different sets of measurements for height, width and length.

Make sure that all sides are correctly measured so that the correct sides correspond. Again, there are seven tabs.

Triangular prism

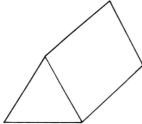

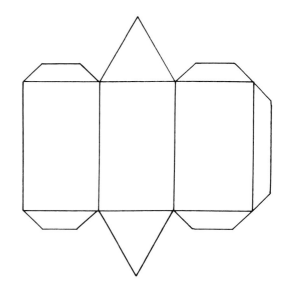

Adjust the size of the triangles and the lengths of the sides as required.

The net shown is for an equilateral triangle.

Cone

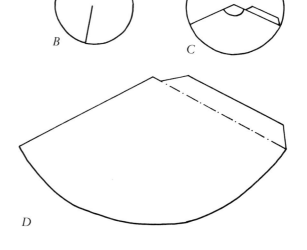

With the cylinder this is, perhaps, the most useful shape in paper sculpture.

The cone is based on a circle, cut along one radius (see *B*) and overlapped. The more overlap there is, the more upright the cone will be (see *A*).

To conserve card and prevent the solid from becoming too bulky, use only part of a circle, as shown in the net (*D*).

For a cone without a point, use the lower part of a circle (as in *C*).

Joining solids

Join solids by fixing one directly on to another or insert one into another, as shown in the diagram.

 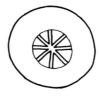 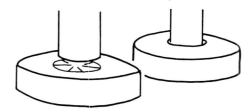

Alternatively, cut a 'star' in the face of one solid and glue the second solid into the hole, using the 'star' pieces as tabs.

Angled cylinders

A good way of making arms is to use a fairly slim cylinder. Roll the card round a felt pen or pencil for support.

Cut a 'V' shape half way down the cylinder, bend the tube towards the 'V' and glue to hold.

Shape the top by cutting away part of the tube and gluing directly on to the body.

A piece of card cut in the shape of a hand may then be glued inside the hand end of the cylinder.

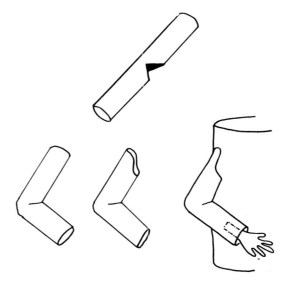

Heads

Make a straight or slightly tapered cylinder and draw the face directly on to the front. Snip tabs around the top of the head and fold these down so that a top can be added.

Alternatively, make the head and neck in two separate pieces and glue head to back of neck. This allows scope for shaping the chin and gives a more three-dimensional effect.

Decorate the head with fringed card for hair, eyebrows, moustache, etc.

TEMPLATES FOR PAPER SCULPTURE HOG

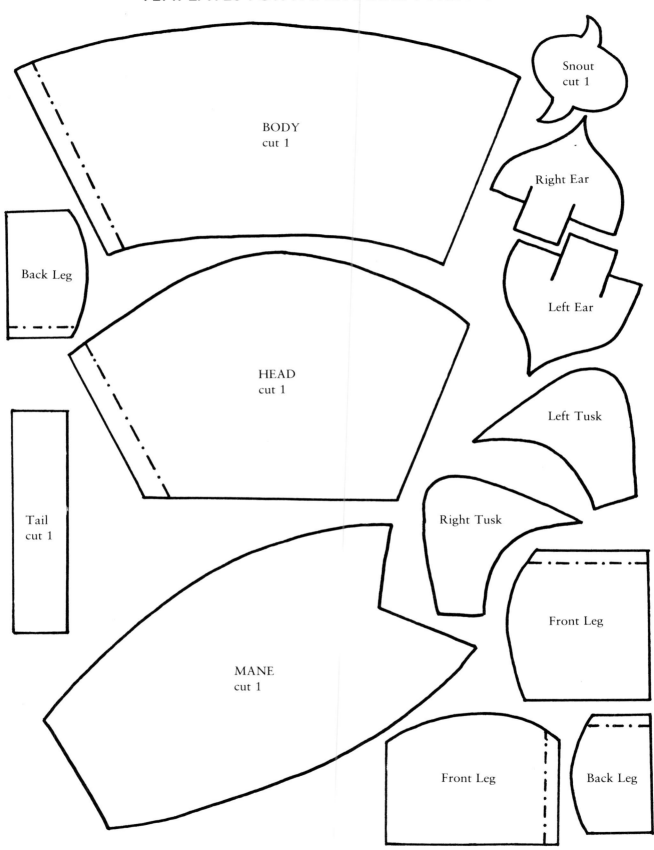

5 Silhouettes

Silhouettes, in miniature, were very popular in Victorian times and are named after the Frenchman who perfected the technique. As it is virtually impossible to copy one's own profile (except by using a photograph) you will need help with Stage 2.

Materials required
A LARGE SHEET OF WHITE PAPER
PENCIL
SCISSORS
BLACK PAINT
A LARGE PAINTBRUSH
A LAMP
SELLOTAPE
MOUNTING PAPER
GLUE

METHOD

1. With small pieces of sellotape, fix the sheet of white paper to the wall and set up the lamp so that, when you stand between it and the paper, the paper catches the shadow of your head and shoulders.

2. Ask someone to draw your shadow, while you stand very still. (You can sit on a chair, if this will help.)

3. Finish the lower part of the outline by drawing a line which sweeps upwards from your chest to the back of your shoulder.

4. Fill in the whole shape with black paint, being extremely careful of the edges, as this can change your profile!

5. Allow the painting to dry completely before continuing.

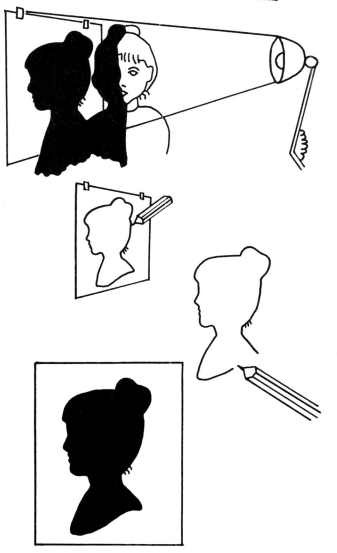

ORGANISING YOUR MATERIALS

I. Setting up the work area

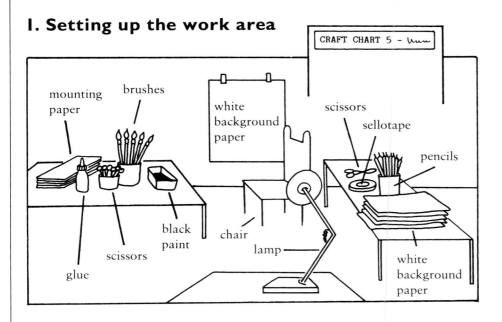

You will need plenty of space for this craft, especially as it will involve a piece of electrical equipment. Ensure that the lamp's flex is directed in a safe manner and not running across the centre of the work area where students could trip over it.

It is suggested that two areas be created, one 'dry' for the drawing of the silhouettes and the other 'wet' area for painting. These do not have to be next to each other – not even in the same room – but do allow plenty of space for moving about.

To cut down on movement, the leader could be responsible for the first stage and actually do the drawing, and then send each student to the painting table to complete the task. This first stage can even be done at some time when other work is going on so that students go to the leader, one at a time, and all the outlines are ready for painting during the designated session.

2. Lamp

An ordinary table lamp, minus the shade, is quite adequate to throw a reasonable shadow. However, quite a lot of adjustment is needed to make sure the height and distance are right to produce a good shadow. An anglepoise or other adjustable lamp is preferable, as this can easily be adjusted to suit the individual.

It is not necessary to black out the room although, of course, this may produce a sharper outline and will add to the excitement of the task.

3. Background paper

White paper is best for the initial drawing as the shadow will show up well on a white background. However, the profile can also be drawn directly on to a piece of brightly coloured craft paper, providing that the outline thrown by the lamp is definite enough.

4. Paint

Silhouettes are, traditionally, black but there is no reason why students should not branch out into other colours, especially if the finished work is to form a frieze where the profiles will overlap.

Powder paint mixed with a generous amount of PVA adhesive is probably the most economical medium to use for this stage. The paint should be thick to give a good covering and there should be plenty of it as the students will use quite a lot for each silhouette. The addition of a PVA medium gives body to the paint and also helps to prevent the dried paint from coming off on fingers and clothing. Handling a large area of dried water-based paint can be a very messy business.

Mixing the paint in a container with a lid will enable it to be stored for future use. If the paint and water separate through standing, just stir well before using again.

5. Glue

PVA glue, which dries to a transparent bond, is ideal for any kind of paper craft. Use a nozzled pot, if possible, and encourage students who have cut their silhouettes to run a narrow line of the adhesive approximately $\frac{1}{2}$–1 cm from the edge of their work. Once the silhouette has been placed in position on the background paper, it is advisable to cover the work with a sheet of paper before running hands over the surface to press it down. Failing that, a gentle pat all round the edge, with the fingertips, should keep it in place.

Glazing – A very effective glaze can be made with PVA adhesive which will give paper a plastic-looking coating. Mix 1 part PVA with 3 parts water and mix well. Cover the work surface with newspaper and place the work to be glazed in the centre. Using a large brush and slow, even strokes, cover the entire surface of the work, right over the edges. At this stage you will be horrified with the result and convinced that it is irreparably damaged. Do not worry, just carefully lift it to a clean sheet of newspaper and allow it to dry completely. This method can be used with any painting but please note that the work should be completely dry before attempting to glaze in this manner and also that paint which has been used for the work may 'run' under the glaze if PVA adhesive was not added to the original paint mixtures. Use a thicker mixture of glaze (1:2) if a more substantial coating is required.

6. Mounting the finished silhouettes

There is a wide variety of choice for displaying the finished work:

(a) *Borders* – Cut strips of black paper (approximately 6 cm in width) which will fit the perimeter of the white paper on which the silhouette has been painted. Mitre each corner (i.e. cut each end to an angle of 45 degrees) so that they join neatly when stuck in place.

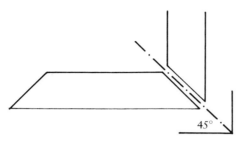

Alternatively, for quickness, cut the strips of paper to fit the sides of the work and leave the corners square. These look perfectly all right from a distance and can save a lot of time if one person has a batch of pictures to mount and time is limited.

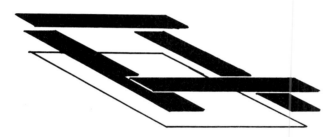

(b) *Mount* – This gives a more professional finish but takes time and a lot of care to ensure neatness.

Cut a background board of fairly thick card to which the finished picture should be affixed.

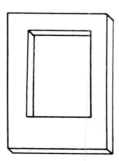

Cut a second board, the same size, which is to be the front mount of the picture. Carefully measure a border inside this card, of the width required. Most professional framers will allow $1\frac{1}{2}$ times the width for the lower border, e.g. if your frame is measured at 5 cm width around the top and sides, allow 7.5 cm for the lower border. Draw this frame on the card with a pencil.

Using a sharp craft knife, metal-edged rule and working on a protected surface, cut through the mounting card where you have marked. Be extremely careful at each corner in order to prevent 'over-cutting' as this will spoil the finished effect. It is advisable to turn the mount for each side so that the rule always sits on the mount side of the cut to protect it from any false cuts which may be made (see diagram).

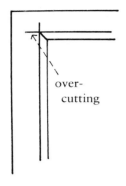

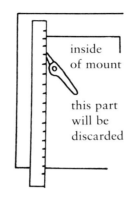

Complete the mounting by gluing the frame to the front of the picture. For a 'special' finish, draw a line in gold or black approximately 0.5 cm from the inside edge all round the mount.

(c) *Mobile* – Use card instead of white background paper and draw and paint the silhouette as described earlier. When the paint has dried, cut out the profile and paint the back as well. Each side, in turn, can be glazed, if required and, when dry, a thread may be attached to the top of the head so that the silhouette can be suspended from the ceiling.

Displaying silhouettes in this way can be great fun, especially in a classroom where children can have their own profiles suspended over their seats.

(d) *Frieze* – Students should complete their work and cut out the dry silhouettes. These can then be mounted on a frieze either side-by-side or overlapping. If it is intended to overlap them, it is advisable to use different-coloured paints as some of the profiles will be lost, from a distance, if they are all painted in black. For a quick frieze, use an assortment of coloured sugar papers on which to draw the profiles, cut them out, without painting them, and mount them on the background frieze as required.

Children always show great enthusiasm for trying to guess who is who – and it is always a lot easier than one might think.

(e) *Miniatures* – The Victorians produced their silhouettes framed ornately and in miniature. It is possible to create your own miniature silhouette by using the method of reduction.

This is done by way of two grids – a large one which will cover the original, life-size profile and one containing the same number of squares but very much smaller.

Start by drawing the outline as already shown, but instead of painting it draw a grid over it of, say, 5-cm squares, Label the columns across the top A, B, C, D, etc. and the rows 1, 2, 3, and so on.

Draw another grid with the same number of squares but making them, say, 0.5 cm each. Label these squares to correspond exactly with the larger grid.

Working logically across the rows, copy the exact shape of any line in square A1 on the large grid, to the same position in square A1 on the small grid. Try to ignore the complete shape of the profile and treat each square individually and in a logical sequence.

When the small profile is completed, transfer it to clean paper by using a sheet of carbon or other transferring device. Finish off as described earlier.

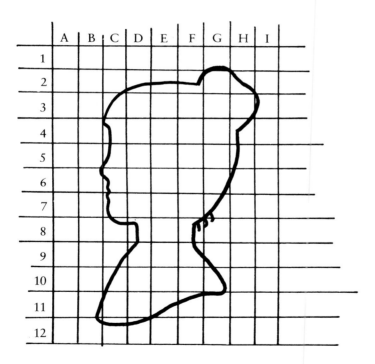

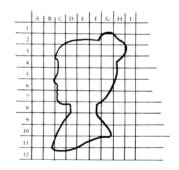

6 Pom-pom Badges

These little badges are very popular with children and give plenty of scope for individuality. The basic technique of pom-pom making is a useful tool in many other crafts.

Materials required
A PIECE OF CARD
SCISSORS
PVA GLUE
PENCIL
ODDMENTS OF WOOL
A SAFETY PIN
A BODKIN
FELT PENS

METHOD

1. Draw and cut out two circles from card and cut out the circles in the centres.

2. Holding the two cards together and using three or four strands of wool at once, wind the wool through the centre hole and around the cards.

3. Continue winding until *half* the circle has been covered. Begin winding back again, over the same half of the circle, as evenly as possible, until the centre hole is completely full. (The bodkin may help you to pull the wool through the hole during the final stages.)

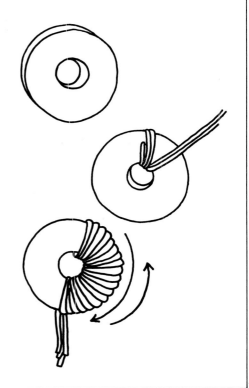

Pom-Pom

4.

When the hole is full, hold the centre firmly and cut the wool around the edge, inserting the scissors between the two cards.

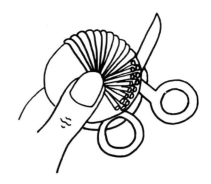

5. Slide two strands of wool between the cards and tie firmly, at the front, to hold the wool together.

6. Tear the cards to the centre and remove them.

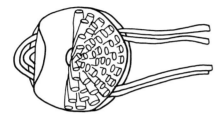 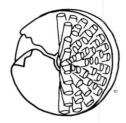

7. Cut a small circle from card. Fold it in half and cut two very small slits. Open the card and thread the back of the safety pin through.

8. Stick the card containing the safety pin to the back of the pom-pom.

9. Make the face, arms, legs, etc. from small pieces of card. Colour and outline them and fix them into the wool with glue. Trim any uneven strands so that the surface is uniform.

Variations

Animals
Use a contrasting colour of wool to tie at Stage 5 and leave the ends long. These can be used to form whiskers and trimmed to the required length.

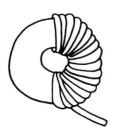 All one colour =  plain pom-pom

Bees

Use yellow and black wool and wind in alternate layers – first layer black, second layer yellow, etc. This will give horizontal stripes when the pom-pom is tied. (Turn pom-pom for vertical stripes – for a tiger, perhaps.)

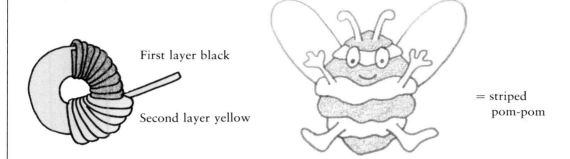

First layer black

Second layer yellow

= striped pom-pom

Humpty-Dumpty

Use two contrasting colours, winding one colour at the top quarter of the circle and the other colour on the bottom quarter. This will give a pom-pom with top and bottom in different colours. Use one colour for the head and the other for the trousers.

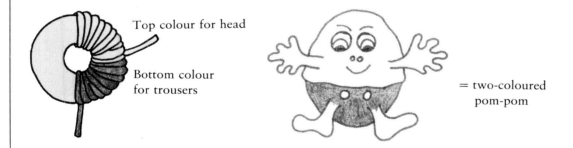

Top colour for head

Bottom colour for trousers

= two-coloured pom-pom

Spiders

Use only one colour, and decorate with eyes and mouth, if required.

Thread four coloured pipe-cleaners through the tied centre so that they stick out either side. Bend each leg to the shape and direction required.

Make up as a badge, or mount in one of the following ways:

(a) Suspend the spider from the ceiling using shirring elastic, so that it bounces.

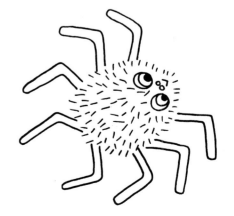

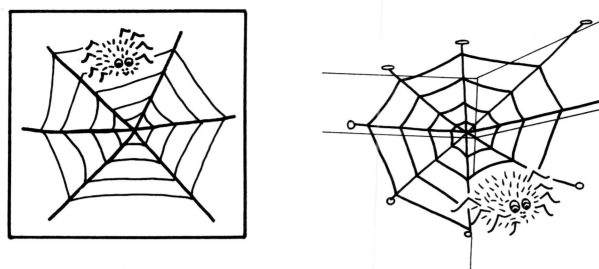

(b) Mark out a web on a sheet of coloured sugar paper. Using white thread, sew the web with long stitches. Fix the spider to the web.

(c) Use thin string to erect free-standing webs in the corners of the room. Spiders can be positioned where required.

ORGANISING YOUR MATERIALS

I. Setting up the work area

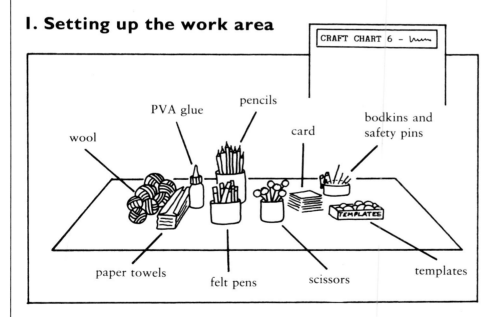

2. Wool

Any ply of wool may be used. It is suggested that students work with three or four strands at once. This will help the work to grow quickly as there is nothing more boring than winding wool round card, one strand at a time.

3. Templates

Prepare templates from the pattern at the end of this chapter or have pairs of compasses available for students to choose their own sizes. Proportion is not crucial, but the diameter of the hole may be as much as one-quarter of the complete diameter.

4. Glue

Use PVA adhesive which dries to a transparent finish so that any 'messy' work will stand a good chance of looking reasonable when it is dry.

Only one glue pot should be necessary. As so little glue is needed, it can be decanted for each child, a small drop at a time, on a paper towel. Children can use an offcut of card as a spreader to apply the glue to the card shapes.

5. Bodkin/weaving needle

Children should be encouraged to pack the ring with as much wool as possible. This will ensure that the finished pom-pom is plump and springy. However, in the latter stages of filling the card rings, it does become quite difficult to get the wool through the hole. For this reason it is suggested that pulling the strands through with a bodkin, or similar instrument, may help to pack the pom-pom tightly.

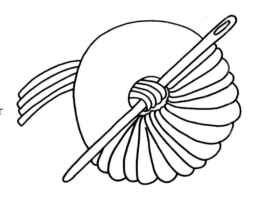

6. Card

Do not use 'best' card for this work. Old swimming/sports day certificates are quite good enough. The only card which will be kept is the small circle stuck to the back of the badge and the oddments used for eyes, ears, hands, etc., which will have been coloured.

The easiest way to cut out the templates is to fold the card in half and cut out both halves at the same time. This dispenses with the need to insert scissors and cut a star in order to cut out the centre hole.

TEMPLATES FOR POM-POMS

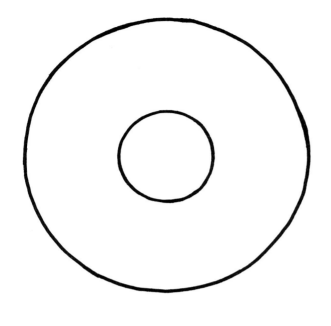

Trace or photocopy this complete circle and transfer it to card so that children have a template from which to cut their own circles. Remember that, using this shape, they will need to insert the scissors in the centre and cut a star in order to remove the centre ring.

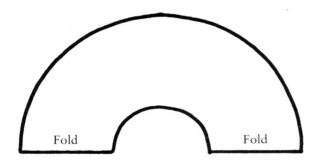

Fold   Fold

Alternatively, copy the above semi-circular shape but remind students that they must fold their piece of card and place the lines marked onto the fold. In this way, both halves of the ring can be cut out in one go and the central circle is easier to remove.

7 Clay Owl Money Box

These money boxes are based on the pinch-pot method of pottery. Use the technique described to turn your model into any type of animal or figure – a pig, a monster, your brother (!) – or omit the money slit and just make a model.

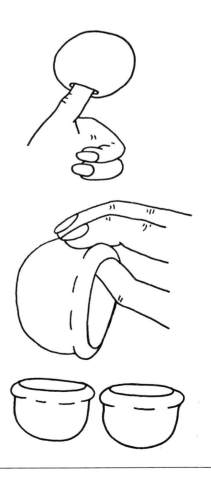

METHOD

1. Take a small lump of clay and smooth it into a round ball. Plunge your thumb into the centre.

2. With your thumb in the middle and two fingers on the outside, begin to pinch the pot to even out the clay. Begin at the bottom and support it in one hand while you turn it round and round, gradually working upwards towards the rim. Feel the thickness of the clay between your thumb and fingers and make it as even as possible.

3. Work only until the top joint of your thumb begins to appear at the edge. You must leave a thick ridge of clay at the top, so *do not touch the rim*.

4. Cover the pot with polythene and set aside. Make another pot in the same way.

5. Gently place the two rims together and cradle the 'egg' in one hand. Use the side of your index finger to slide clay from the thick rims into the hollow join so that no gap shows. Try not to press too hard or your 'egg' will collapse.

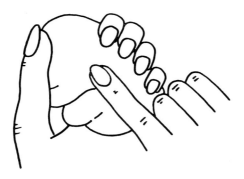

6. When the join has disappeared, work round and round the shape, stroking the clay to smoothness. The more you stroke, the smoother it will become.

7. Stand your finished 'egg' on the work surface and decorate as required

Important points to remember

There are three methods you can use to decorate your 'egg'. You can add more clay to the shape; you can cut away some of the existing clay; you can press your modelling tool into the clay to make patterns in it.

(a) *Adding more clay*

For wings, ears, eyes, tails, etc. pieces of clay can be shaped and added to the body. Remember that if these are just placed in position they will eventually dry out and fall away. For this reason it is essential that all pieces to be added should be made slightly larger than you need them to be. This will give you plenty of clay to smooth down on to the model so that the piece is completely 'keyed-in' all round, with no join showing. Even small eyes should be attached firmly in this way or they will fall out when the model is dry.

(b) *Cutting away existing clay*

You will be using this method for making the money slit and the hole in the base for the money to come out.

Lightly mark out the area to be removed and, using the modelling tool, gradually work at the clay to remove it a small piece at a time. Try to work in a sideways direction so as not to push it inwards. Remember that the 'egg' is hollow and will need support if pressure is to be applied.

(c) *Making patterns*
Carefully press your modelling tool (or any other instrument) into the clay to leave a shape. Again, remember to give the model support and not to press too hard. Feathers and hair can be very effective if done in this way.

8. To make the money slit

When you are satisfied with your model, mark a double line at the back of the head, where you wish the slit to be. Using the modelling tool, gradually work at this section, lifting out the clay piece by piece until the slit goes right through to the hollow inside.

Ensure that the slit is big enough to take the size of coin you wish to save.

Smooth down all the rough edges.

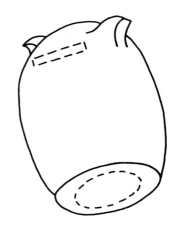

9. To make the hole in the base

Mark out a circle on the base of your model which is big enough to allow all your money to come out!

Use the same method as above to remove the circle and, again, smooth down all rough edges.

10. Allow the model to dry enough so that you can hold and press it without spoiling its shape.

11. Making the stand and claws

(a) Take a small ball of clay and flatten it to form a base. It should be thick and about the same size as the base of your model.

(b) Press the base of your model into the clay disc and trim round it. When you lift your model up, you will find that the fresh clay has risen in the centre to form a 'bung' in the hole.

(c) Smooth down all rough edges and add claws to the front of the disc, remembering Important Point (a) above.

(d) Allow both parts (body and base) to dry out separately.

12. When the model is completely dry and has changed colour, paint and varnish it. Do allow both parts to dry out completely before putting them together.

ORGANISING YOUR MATERIALS

1. Setting up the work area

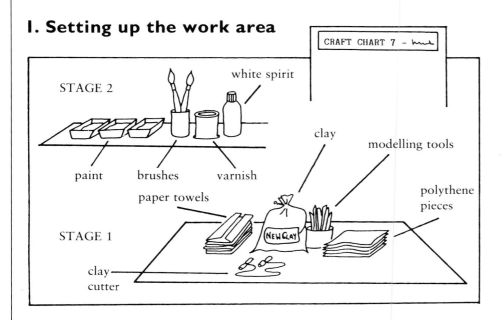

CRAFT CHART 7 –

STAGE 2

white spirit

paint　　brushes　　varnish

clay

modelling tools

paper towels

polythene pieces

STAGE 1

NEW CLAY

clay cutter

Work on an easy-clean surface and wipe table after use with warm water and washing-up liquid.

2. Clay

Many schools possess kilns these days, and this piece of craftwork may be completed by glazing the money box instead of using paint and varnish. However, the item was included with self-hardening clay in mind, so as not to exclude any group of youngsters, whether they be at school, in a cub/brownie group, or even pursuing a hobby at home by themselves.

Most craft shops stock self-hardening clay in kilo bags, at a reasonable cost. The larger educational suppliers also stock this medium.

The clay will last in store for a considerable time, but once the bag is opened the clay will begin to harden, if left open to the air. To conserve the clay and keep it workable for as long as possible, ensure that it is well covered in polythene and returned to its bag in as airtight a condition as possible. It must also be protected *during use*, especially on warm days or if the work is being done in a centrally heated room.

The clay comes from the manufacturer wrapped in a thin membrane of polythene and inside a thick polythene bag. It is suggested that the medium be taken out of the thick bag and placed on the table for

use but that the thin membrane is left in place and only pulled back as each piece of clay is needed. Students should be made aware that, if they take a piece of clay, they should re-cover the rest of the clay in order to protect it from the air.

After use, return the clay to the thick bag and extract as much air as possible. The neck can be twisted and resealed with the wire twist clip provided. Store in a cool place.

3. Clay cutter

Although not essential, a clay cutter is a very useful piece of equipment and very easy to make.

Use two toggle buttons (or pieces of wood) and tie a length of fishing line between them. The implement can be used to slice through the clay, and it is far easier to use than trying to gouge handfuls of clay out of a large lump.

If using self-hardening clay, it will be noticed that, when cut, it leaves tiny hairs on the fishing line. This is because it contains minute nylon fibres which help to bond the medium when dry. This can be explained to the students and a section of clay cut with the cutter to show them the fibres. Some students may wish to use the fibre to decorate their finished work, as it makes quite good moustaches and eyebrows!

4. Clay modelling tools

Sets of tools can be purchased from any craft shop or supplier. However, any type of instrument can be used, from an old biro to a lolly-stick – in fact anything which will give an interesting pattern. The best tool for smoothing down clay is a finger. The oil from one's skin gives a polished surface to the clay.

5. Polythene pieces

Cut up some old carrier bags and keep them readily available. They come in very useful during the session, for wrapping up small pieces of clay to prevent them from drying out while waiting to be used.

If, at the end of the session, some models still need to have work done on them and are not ready to be left open to the air, they can be wrapped in a piece of polythene and kept as airtight as possible so that the clay is still workable for the next session.

Any model, or part of the model, which is not going to be used for a while, should be wrapped in polythene to prevent premature drying.

6. Paper towels

These are always a useful item to have during a 'messy' craftwork session. Students can use a paper towel to stand their work on and this will cut down the amount of mess on the work surface.

7. Water

Do not use water with self-hardening clay. Potters use a lot of water in their trade and, with natural clay which is to be fired in the kiln, water is necessary to keep a working consistency. However, if it is applied to self-hardening clay in any quantity, the work will turn in to a primeval sludge and become quite unmanageable. The surface will also be spoiled and show a very powdery finish when it has dried out.

Despite the above comments, it is sometimes useful to moisten very small areas which show signs of drying and still need to be worked. Use only one finger, dipped in water, and apply this direct to that part of the surface that requires attention.

It is far better, and easier, to protect the clay and keep it in a moist condition than to try to 'reclaim' it once the drying process has started.

8. Paint

If using self-hardening clay, a normal powder or ready-mix paint can be used to colour the model. Add a generous squeeze of PVA glue to the paint before use as this will help to prevent the colours running into one another when the varnish is applied.

If using a clay which requires firing, this can also be painted after the initial biscuit fire, but if glazes are available the work can be completed with coloured glazes and fired again.

9. Varnish

When the paint is completely dry, use a polyurethane varnish to complete the work. Begin with all white areas, then light colours and finally the browns and blacks. This will also ensure that dark paint does not discolour the lighter areas.

Leave the two sections (body and feet) to dry separately and do not be tempted to put them together until the varnish is really dry (approximately 24 hours).

8 Spiro-Lites

This 'mobile' toy has a fascination for adults and children alike. Change the planes to birds or spaceships of your own design.

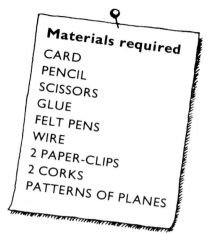

Materials required
CARD
PENCIL
SCISSORS
GLUE
FELT PENS
WIRE
2 PAPER-CLIPS
2 CORKS
PATTERNS OF PLANES

METHOD

1. Colour two sets of planes, A and B.

2. From set A, cut out 1 *body*, 1 *large wing* and 1 *small wing*. Glue them to card and cut them out carefully.

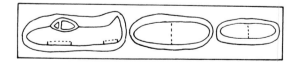

3. Snip the flaps marked on the body and fold them upwards.

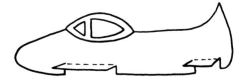

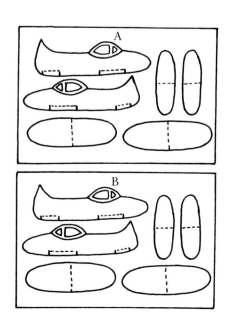

4. Cut out the remainder of the plane. Snip the flaps on the body and fold upwards, and glue the pieces into place on the second side of the card.

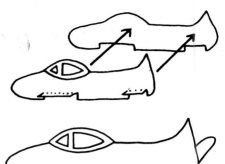

5. Glue the wings to the body, under the flaps.

6. Make the second plane B in the same way.

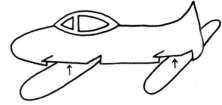

7. Cut a length of wire, approximately 20 cm and bend it into shape for the cross-piece. Keep the arms as even as possible to ensure good balance.

8. Use a paper-clip to attach one plane to each end of the cross-piece and bend the wire over to prevent the planes falling off.

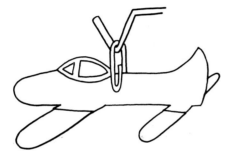

9. Cut a length of wire approximately 32 cm and wind it round the barrel of a felt pen to form a spring.

Remove the pen carefully and, holding one end in each hand, gently pull the spring open to form a spiral. Be very gentle or you may damage the flow of the coil and your planes will not fly smoothly.

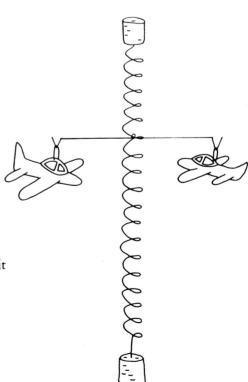

10. Straighten the last 2 cm at both ends of the spiral and push *one* end into a cork.

11. Thread the cross-piece on to the open end of the spiral and then fit a cork to this end also.

Hold the spiral vertically, with the planes at the top and they should spin down the spiral to the bottom. Adjust the coil if necessary.

For a 'return trip', simply turn the spiral upside down so that the planes are again at the top.

ORGANISING YOUR MATERIALS

I. Setting up the work area

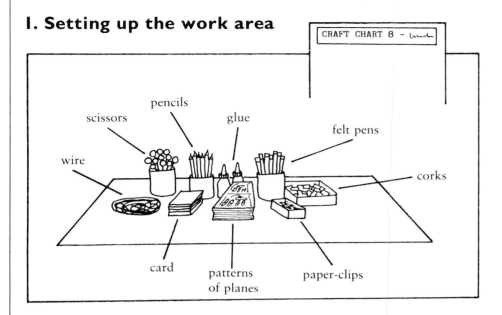

CRAFT CHART 8 –

scissors
pencils
glue
felt pens
wire
corks
card
patterns of planes
paper-clips

2. Card

There is no need to use 'best' card, as it will all be covered by the coloured planes. Old manila folders or scrap pieces are quite adequate.

If using large sheets of card, it can be conserved by cutting it to size (13.5 cm squares) before the session starts. Children will need two pieces of card this size to complete the planes.

3. Patterns

Photocopy the patterns at the end of this chapter so that each child has a Set A and Set B ready to begin. It is suggested that they start with the colouring for two reasons. It is far easier to colour and outline the planes while they are still on the large sheet than to try to hold them steady for colouring once they have been cut out. Also, children will be enthusiastic to begin putting their individual 'stamp' on the paper and it makes for a calm and efficient beginning to the session. It will also give the organiser time to tidy up any loose ends of preparation necessary.

Accuracy in cutting out is fairly important when making up the planes and, obviously, the more times the planes are cut out the more chance there is for errors to be magnified. Therefore, suggest to the children that, once they have coloured the planes, they 'rough-cut' the piece required from the sheet and stick it to card, leaving the more detailed cutting of the exact shape until they can cut out pattern and card together. This will eliminate at least one cut where inaccuracies may occur.

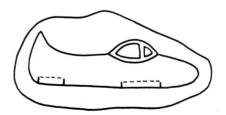

4. Glue

White PVA adhesive, which becomes transparent when dry, is a good medium to use. However, if a large group is working and the glue has been decanted into small pots, spreaders (or offcuts of card used as spreaders) will be needed so that the glue can be applied thinly. If too much glue is put on, the work will become untidy and take a long time to dry. If children are using nozzled pots of glue, encourage them to hold the nozzle right down on the paper and squeeze gently. This will allow only a thin line of glue to be administered. (Remember that it is easier to add a bit more glue than spend time trying to scrape it off.)

5. Wire

Although no particular gauge of wire is recommended here, choose one which will hold its shape when in use but which is not too stiff for the children to handle comfortably. A small pair of wire cutters or pliers should be available during the session. From experience I have found that it is much more satisfactory to have ready-cut lengths of wire (hence the 'short' and 'long' wires which appear on the craft chart). This does require more preparation but means that children do not have to wait in a queue to use the wire cutters – a practice not recommended anyway where young children are involved.

It is important that the wire cross-piece, from which the planes are suspended, is kept as symmetrical as possible, for this will affect the balance and smoothness of the flight. To help children to keep these arms of an even length, make a pattern board which can be used to bend the wire to shape.

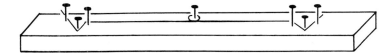

Using a ruler and red pen, draw the shape of the wire on to an offcut of wood. Hammer in seven nails, as shown in the diagram. The red line will show the path of the wire and on which side of each nail it should lie.

Children can use the pattern board, following the red line through the nails, to give a balanced cross-piece section.

6. Corks

Corks are always useful in craftwork and can be collected by the group, or by an individual, for use at some future time.

Children will need two corks each for this piece of work or, if there are few corks, cut one cork in two, crosswise, so that one half can be used at the top of the spiro-lite and the other half at the bottom.

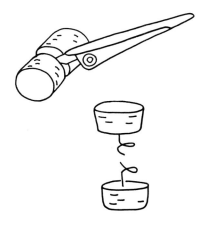

As the job of the corks is simply to prevent the planes from falling off at the end of each flight, this job could be done with any type of substitute (plasticine, sellotape or by folding the wire back on itself) but corks certainly do look best.

TEMPLATES FOR SPIRO-LITES

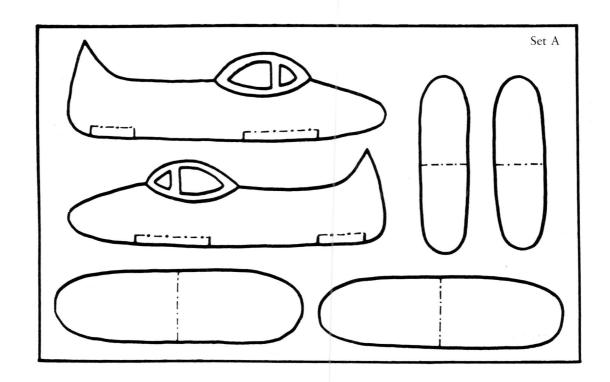

Set A

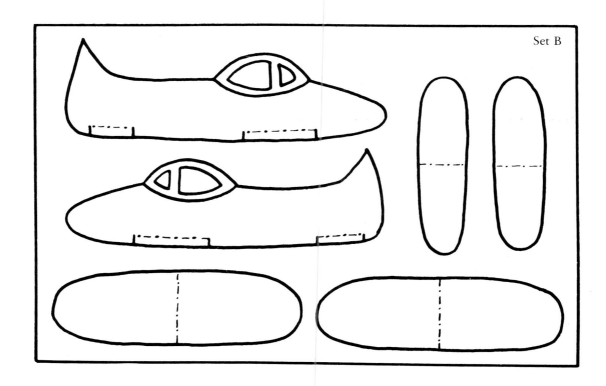

Set B

9 Masks

These three-dimensional masks are based on a helmet design which is both comfortable to wear and unlikely to slip or fall off. They are very effective for school productions, plays and assemblies.

Materials required
CARD
PENCIL
SCISSORS
PVA GLUE
STAPLER (optional)
PAINTING EQUIPMENT
TEMPLATE(S)

METHOD (the basic mask)

1. On a piece of card, draw round the template of the basic mask shape, the side and top bands. Don't forget to draw round the eye holes, too.

Cut them out carefully.

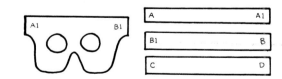

2. Attach the two side bands (marked A1 and B1) to the sides of the mask.

3. Attach the top band (D) to the centre top of the mask.

Use glue or a stapler for fixing the bands, but if using staples ensure that the flat side of the staple is *inside* the mask. Otherwise, the legs of the staples will catch your hair as you put the mask on and off and this can be a painful and off-putting experience.

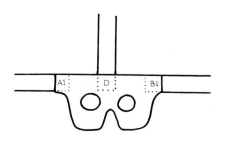

4. Place the mask against your face so that you can see through the eye holes and the mask feels comfortable.

5. Smooth the bands round and over your head so that they meet at the back. Then, holding the three bands tightly together, carefully remove the mask and fix the bands together. Cut off any surplus band which sticks out.

6. Decorate the basic mask shape or cut more card to turn your mask into one of the following birds or animals.

Bird

1. Choose a beak from the templates at the end of the chapter, and draw round it on a piece of card.

2. Score along all the dotted lines.

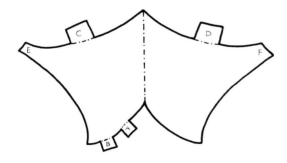

3. Turn tabs A and B in and fold the whole beak in half along the centre scored line.

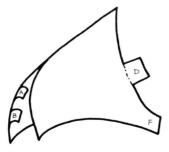

4. Use a *small* dab of glue on tabs A and B to join the curve of the beak.

5. Fold tabs C and D inwards.

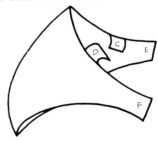

6. Open the beak, and glue tabs C and D to the basic mask, just under the eyes.

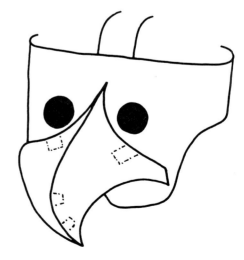

7. Glue points E and F to the cheeks of the basic mask.

Decorate the bird.

Suggestions

Paint and glaze the beak before making it up. A line drawn from the tip to the centre of points E and F (on the straight beak) will give the impression of a lower jaw.

Use pieces of card or tissue paper cut to the shape of feathers. These can be fixed to the mask to give a more three-dimensional effect.

Monkey

1. Take the templates for the monkey's face and ears. Draw round them on to a piece of card and cut them out.

2. Score along all the dotted lines.

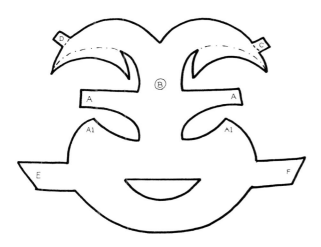

3. Ease the eyebrows into shape by curving the card as you fold along the scored line.

4. Glue the tabs marked A to the underside of the areas A1 to form the nostrils.

5. Anchor point B to the centre front of the basic mask, between the eyes.

6. Glue tabs C and D to the sides of the mask to make the forehead.

7. Push the face upwards and attach tabs E and F to the cheeks of the basic mask so that the muzzle protrudes.

8. Make up the ears by overlapping side X on to side Y – ensure that you make a matching pair. Fold back tabs G and H and glue these to the sides of the head, fairly low down.

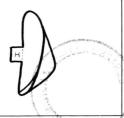

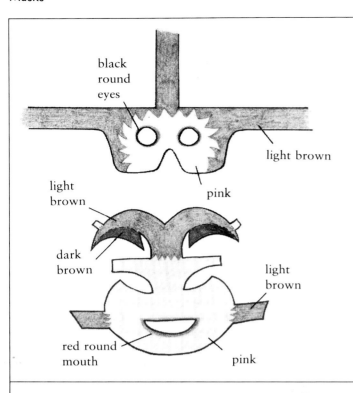

black round eyes

light brown

light brown

pink

dark brown

light brown

red round mouth

pink

Suggestions

The mask can be painted and glazed before being made up. It can even be covered in fur fabric which has been cut to the same pattern as the card.

Outline the eye holes as this will give life to the eyes when the mask is being worn.

pink ears

Frog

1. Take the template for the frog's face and lower jaw. Draw round them on to green card and cut them out.

Draw round the templates for the eyes on to white card and cut these out.

2. Score along all the dotted lines.

3. Working on the large face piece, ease the eyebrows into a curved shape, folding along the scored line.

Ease back the under side of the upper lip, along the scored line and glue the card on to itself, each end at point B. Overlap G and H – glue these to keep a point on the upper lip.

Fix point A to the centre front of the basic mask shape and glue tabs C and D to the basic mask to hold the eyebrows in a deep wide curve. *Do not* fix the upper lip to the basic mask yet.

4. Working on the lower lip, gently fold along the scored line, easing the card into the natural curve. Fold the ends back on themselves at points E and F and glue to hold.

Overlap I and J and glue to a point to match the upper lip.

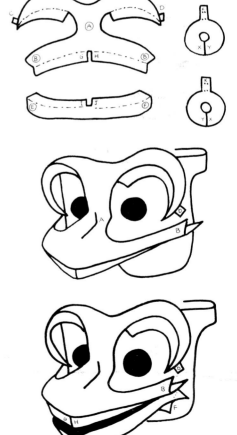

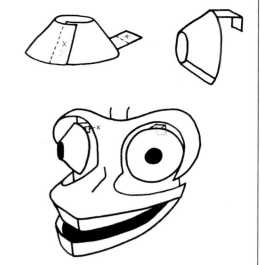

5. At this stage it is best to fit the mask on someone to gauge where the lips should be attached to the basic mask.

Hold the ends of the upper and lower lips together to form a mouth (upper lip on top) and fix the jaw together at each end to give a wide, open mouth. (A stapler is best for this.)

Push the whole mouth upwards so that the 'nose' protrudes and the face bends at point A where it is attached to the mask. Fix the ends of the lips to the basic mask at each side.

6. Make up the eyes by gluing X over Y on both pieces. Fold the tabs along the scored lines and suspend the eyes in the sockets. NB: these eyes should look out 'sideways' to give a 'froggy' appearance. The wearer will look through the basic mask eyes, not the frog's eyes.

Suggestions
Paint and glaze the pieces before making up the mask.
Outline the eyes with a black line both round the edge and at the pupil.

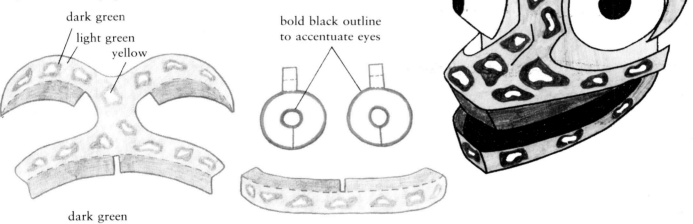

dark green
light green
yellow
bold black outline to accentuate eyes

dark green

Lion

1. Take the templates for the lion, draw round them on to card and cut them out.

2. Score along all the dotted lines.

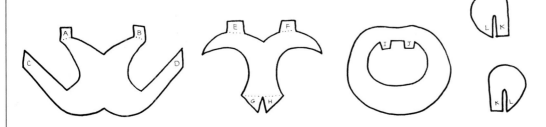

3. The muzzle

Fold tabs A and B over the top of the basic mask and glue into place. Fix points C and D to the cheeks of the basic mask.

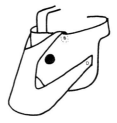

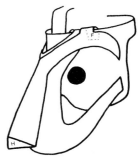

4. The nose

Overlap G and H and glue to hold the nose in a point. Fold tabs E and F over the top of the basic mask and glue in place.

5. The mane

Keep the mane folded in half and fringe the edge as in the diagrams. Cutting both sides at the same time will ensure that the mane looks even and symmetrical.

Glue tabs I and J to the top of the basic mask, behind the eyebrows.

6. The ears

Overlap tab K above tab L and glue to hold. (Ensure that you make a matching pair.)

Glue ears to the top of the basic mask, behind the mane.

7.
Complete the lion's face by adding whisker spots on his cheeks and a red tissue-paper tongue

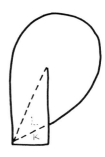

Suggestions

This mask is most effective if made from pastel shades of manila card. Use yellow, orange, buff or pink in any combination.

Offcuts of card can be fringed and added to the mane and basic helmet to make a fuller head of hair.

Complete the costume with a tail of card with a fringed card tassel and fringed card bracelets to match.

Outline the eyes of the basic mask to accentuate the three-dimensional effect.

ORGANISING YOUR MATERIALS

I. Setting up the work area

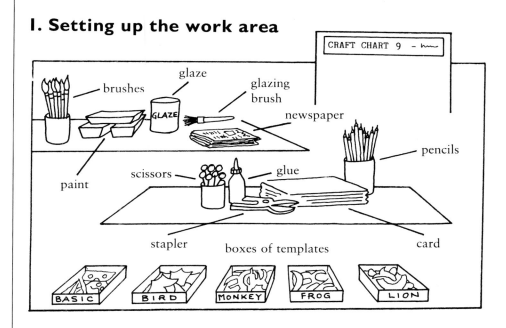

Mask-making sessions can be as easy or as complicated as one cares to make them. They are many variables to be taken into consideration – the age and ability of the students, the availability of the materials and the amount of time which can be spent in preparation. The following suggestions and alternatives may help the organiser to plan a mask-making session within the limits of the circumstances.

2. Templates

The patterns on the last pages of this chapter are produced exactly half size. Either use a photocopier which enlarges to double proportions or use the technique of enlargement by squares. The patterns are produced here on 2.5 cm squares so, to double the size, draw squares of 5 cm dimensions and copy the pattern, square for square (see page 61). A piece of A3 paper will accommodate even the lion's mane, which is the largest piece to reproduce.

The following notes may prove useful to the organiser when deciding which mask to attempt with a group of children.

The bird mask

This is easiest of the four masks, as there is only one piece (the beak) to attach to the basic helmet. It is a useful starting-point for smaller children as it will teach the techniques of cutting to a given line, scoring and the importance of tabs for joining pieces of card. They will gain experience of handling card and moulding it to the shape they want and can then progress to more complicated work.

Here the helmet is an important part of the finished mask as it forms the actual head of the bird, so any painting and glazing should be done on the separate pieces before attempting to build them into a three-dimensional shape (see section on 'Painting and Glazing', p. 60).

There is plenty of scope for individuality in the decoration of the bird, from the budding ornithologist who remains faithful to nature, feather by feather, to the weird and wonderful creations designed by the young science-fiction enthusiast.

Feathers can be made from card, fabric or tissue paper and arranged on the head after the beak has been fixed. Begin with a line of feathers around the edge of the helmet and gradually work inwards, towards the beak and eyes, so that each line of feathers covers the bases of the previous row. Glue the lower edge of each feather only, so as to retain the three-dimensional effect.

If a complete bird's head is required, fix additional bands from one side of the helmet, across the top of the head, to the opposite side. These can be anchored together at the top with a staple (flat side inside to prevent hair-pulling!) and the feathers attached to the extra bands to cover the entire head.

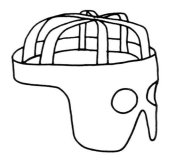

The monkey mask
Again, if the mask is to be painted and glazed, complete this stage before the pieces are put together. The appeal in this design is the way the nostrils join (A tabs glued under A1) and stand out from the helmet. Once the face has been anchored to the helmet at point B, don't be afraid to push the nose upwards so that the side tabs C and D can be fixed to the cheeks of the basic mask. The ears should be fixed fairly low down on the sides of the head to complete the really monkey-looking proportions.

Outlining the eyes on the basic mask will accentuate the three-dimensional effect.

The frog mask
Although there are only a few pieces to this design, it is by far the most complicated of the four masks. Arranging the mouth so that it looks symmetrical and balanced is the part which even some adults may find frustrating. Use a stapler to join the pieces together – they can be readjusted, if necessary, and there is no waiting for glue to dry. Just exercise a little patience and make the card do what *you* want, rather than what *it* wants to do. Gentle persuasion will win through.

If card is scarce and there is none large enough to accommodate the face all in one piece, the pattern may be separated at A (across the 'bridge' of the nose) and cut out in two halves, adding enough extra to join them back again into one piece.

The lion mask
This mask may look complicated but is, in fact, one of the easiest to make. However, as the pieces are large, they will eat into the stock of card.

NB: The mane is the only pattern piece in this chapter to be reproduced in half and needing to be placed on the fold. (Many of the other pieces can be treated this way, if preferred.)

Encourage students to draw the fringing on to the mane before cutting so that this can be checked before they put scissors to the piece. As the mane takes up a large amount of card, cutting it wrongly can be an expensive mistake. If the card available is too small to enable the whole mane to be cut from one piece, cut the two halves from separate cards and allow a little extra on the 'fold' for overlapping the join.

Preparing the templates

Enlarge the patterns at the end of the chapter onto reasonably thick card which will keep its shape when being drawn round. Mark the tabs with the correct letters and show the score lines and other instructions.

The number of templates prepared will depend on the size of the group and the way the organiser intends to plan the session. Try to prepare enough templates – especially of the basic mask – so that students are not kept waiting to begin.

Place the templates in appropriately labelled boxes.

Scoring

Scoring is the process of cutting through the top surface of the card so that it will fold along a controlled line. This is usually done with a craft knife and a light pressure to prevent the cut from going right through the card. It is the only sure method of making the card fold exactly where and in the way that you require. Sharp, straight folds can be made using this method, and practically any type of curve can be obtained, with a little practice. Always use a metal (or metal-edged) rule.

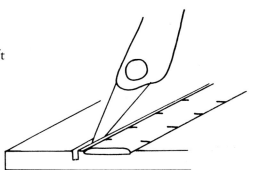

If the idea of letting students loose with craft knives fills you with horror, an adequate alternative is an open pair of scissors. Just run the point of one of the blades along the line to be folded and use a little more pressure than would be necessary with a knife. Remember that it is only the top surface of the card which needs to be marked; it should not be cut right the way through. Practise the technique a few times prior to explaining and demonstrating it to the group.

3. Card

Tinted manila card is ideal for mask-making. This can be purchased in packs of assorted colours from most educational suppliers or obtained by the sheet from art/craft shops (but this can be quite expensive). There is no reason why empty cereal packets cannot be used but this may mean joining some of the larger pattern pieces and students must be aware that some pieces may bend in the wrong place where the sides of the boxes were hinged.

Providing that it is easy to cut and handle, most types of card can be used. To conserve card, the organiser can prepare the masks by drawing round the templates for the students prior to the session. This ensures that the minimum of card is used, but does take time. It is a question of weighing up the importance of saving card against the time available for preparation.

4. Painting and glazing

Although paper sculpture is very effective when the card is left with its natural colouring, a more lifelike effect is obtained if the work is painted.

Paint the individual pattern pieces *before* building them into the three-dimensional shape, as the card will absorb water from the paint and the pieces are far more manageable when laid flat to dry.

Paint

Use a water-based powder paint or ready-mix to which has been added a liberal squeeze of PVA medium. Mix well. The PVA will thicken the paint so that it covers the card in one coat and will bring out the brightness of the colours. It will also give an added resistance to the colours running into each other when the glaze is applied. Outlining the colours in black, where appropriate, will 'lift' them so that they can be seen clearly from a distance. This can be a very useful asset if the masks are to be used in a play and need to be seen from the back of a hall.

Lay out all the pattern pieces on a large sheet of newspaper so that the paint can be taken over all the edges. It is not necessary to paint the inside of the mask. Allow the paint to dry completely before applying the glaze.

Glaze

Use the PVA medium diluted in the proportions 1 part PVA to 3 parts water. Use less water if a thicker coating is required. The beauty of this glaze is that it gives the card a laminated finish which not only shines but also protects the card, giving it a much longer life. (Children's artwork can also be treated in this way to give it a protective coating, providing that the original work will not suffer by 'running' when the glaze is applied.)

NB: When you start applying the glaze, do not be alarmed by thinking that you have ruined the entire piece of work. The glaze will be thick and opaque, cover the painting completely and probably look a thorough mess. However, as PVA dries to a transparent finish, the colours will eventually come through again.

Lay out each painted pattern piece on a sheet of newspaper. Work with a large brush and make as few strokes as possible, working from one side of the piece to the other. Use a light touch so that the brush does not 'scrape' across the paintwork more than is absolutely necessary. Cover the entire pattern piece, working right over the edges. When it is completely covered, it is advisable to release it from the newspaper and move it to a clean sheet so that it does not stick to the newspaper as it is drying.

5. Stapler

These masks can be put together just as well with a stapler as with glue. The younger the children, the more help they will need with arranging the three-dimensional pieces. A stapler is a very useful tool, as less time will be required attending to each individual need. It also means that pieces can be readjusted, if necessary, with the minimum of damage.

A hand-gun type stapler is best as this gives maximum control over the instrument. However, any type or size of stapler can be used, providing that the organiser remembers to fix the staples with the *flat side inside* the mask.

6. Glue

For a more permanent bonding of pieces, use the same PVA medium (undiluted) as was used for the glaze. As already advised, this dries to a transparent finish which will not detract from the paintwork should any be left showing on the outside of the mask.

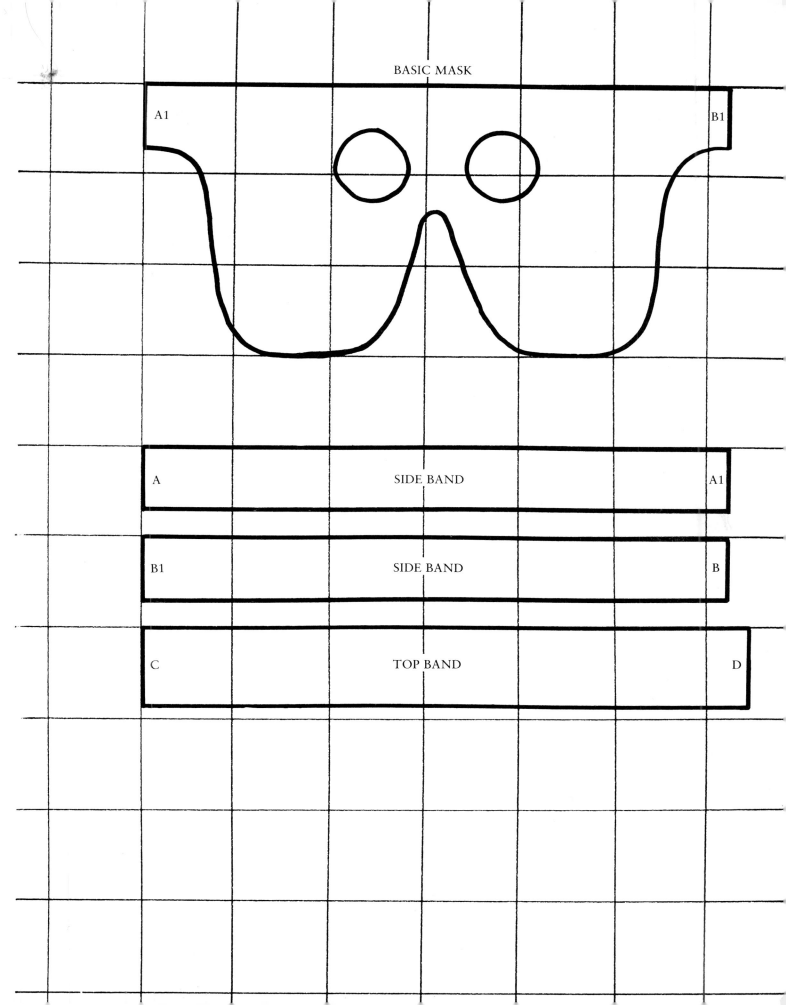

BASIC MASK

A1

B1

A SIDE BAND A1

B1 SIDE BAND B

C TOP BAND D

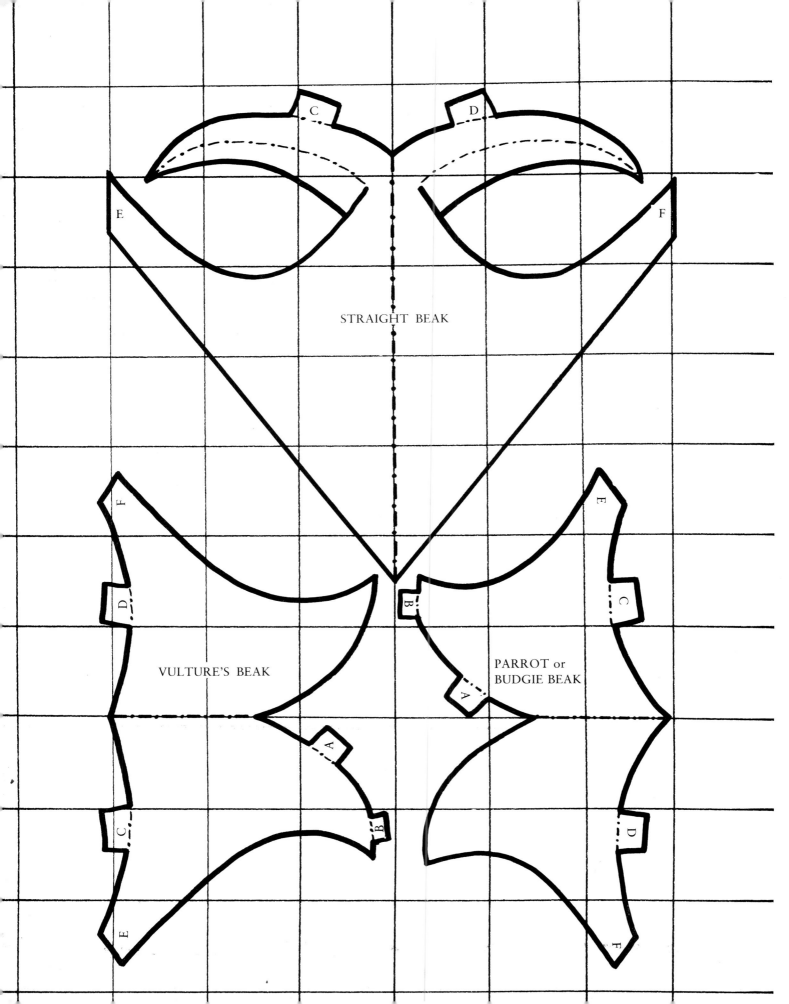

STRAIGHT BEAK

VULTURE'S BEAK

PARROT or
BUDGIE BEAK

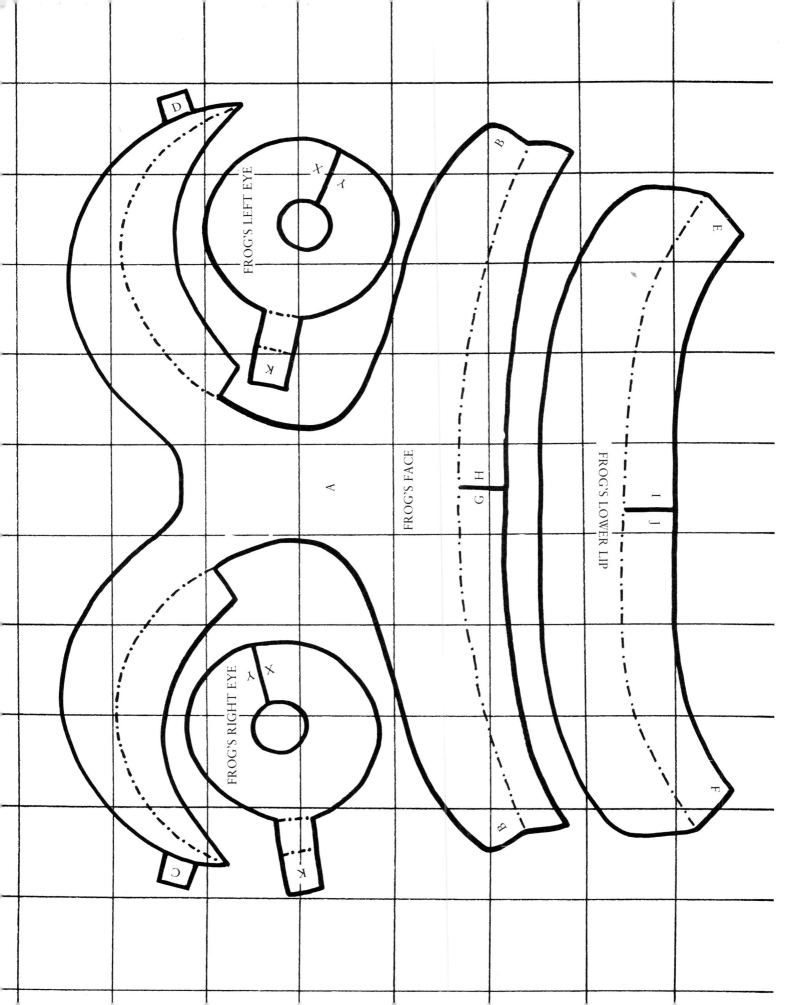

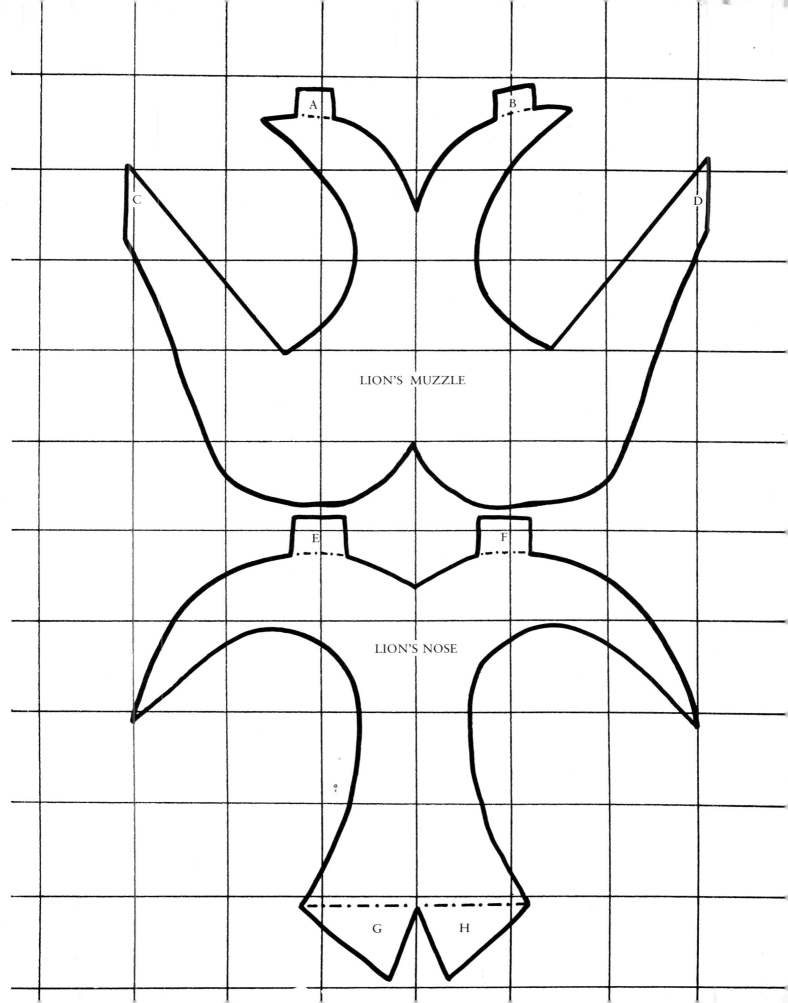

LION'S MUZZLE

LION'S NOSE

10 Papier Mâché Napkin Ring

These napkin rings are inexpensive to make but most effective on the dinner table. They make a delightful gift, complete with napkins. Choose your own colour scheme and design to suit that of the dining-room.

METHOD

1. Tear newspaper and white paper into 1 cm squares and keep them in two separate heaps.

newspaper

white paper

2. With a craft knife, carefully cut the toilet roll middle into quarters so that you have four rings of equal height.

3. Paste the *inside* of one ring with the cold-water paste.

4. With the brush, pick up one piece of newspaper at a time and paste it to the inside of the ring. The pieces should overlap and stick out at the top and bottom of the cardboard.

5. Paste the *outside* of the ring and, using your fingers, carefully fold the newspaper over to the outside to make a neat edge top and bottom.

6. Using the brush again, pick up more pieces of newspaper and fill all the gaps that show on the outside of the ring. Remember to overlap the pieces so that, when you have finished this layer, no cardboard is showing either inside or outside.

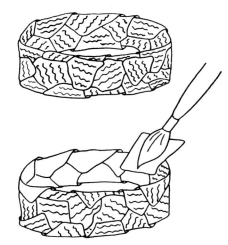

7. Repeat the process of covering the whole ring, inside and out, this time using white paper and keeping the top and bottom rims very smooth.

8. Apply another complete layer of newspaper, followed by another complete layer of white paper.

You should have pasted four layers altogether, ending with a white paper layer.

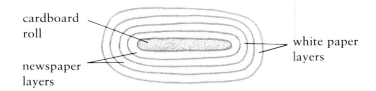

cardboard roll

white paper layers

newspaper layers

9. Now paint a plain inside to the ring and your design or picture on the outside, so that no white paper is left showing.

If you decide to paint immediately, without drawing the pattern first, there is no need to wait for the paste to dry. However, this can be quite messy on the fingers, so have something to wipe them on and also a paper towel to stand the ring on when you need to turn it round.

10. When the paint is quite dry, varnish the ring.

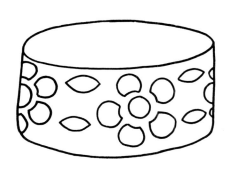

You can make individual rings for special people or a set of four or six, all of the same colour and pattern.

ORGANISING YOUR MATERIALS

I. Setting up the work area

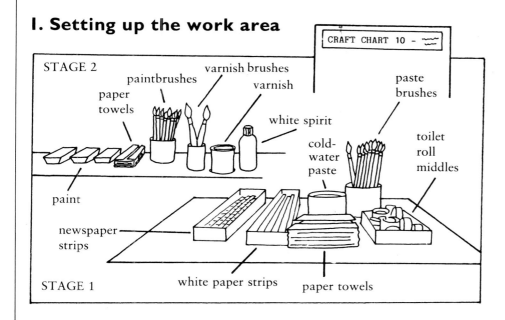

As this piece of craftwork will take longer than one session to complete, it will only be necessary to set up the papier mâché table for the first one, or perhaps two, sessions. Once some students have completed the papier mâché stage, it is advisable to have a separate table set out with the painting materials so that the work surface does not become too crowded with equipment.

2. Toilet roll middles

These are a very useful item to collect for use in craftwork and any art/craft department or group can keep a collection of this type of disposable equipment. If storage space is limited, the rolls can be collected just a few days before the session is due to take place or children can be asked to bring one from home for the session itself. However, children are most unreliable in this respect and there are bound to be some who find it impossible to produce anything from home or who simply 'forget', so have a few spare ones to hand. Kitchen towel, clingfilm and kitchen foil middles are also suitable and, as they are longer than toilet rolls, more rings can be cut from them. However, some of these rolls are of a much smaller diameter than toilet rolls and, although a napkin will still fit inside, they do become rather difficult to work inside when three or four layers of paper are added to the cardboard.

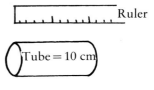

The organiser should do the cutting of the cardboard rolls before the session, so that children do not need to use the craft knife.

Measure the length of the toilet roll and divide it by four to ascertain the height that each ring must be to enable four to be cut from each roll. Draw a rectangle on thick paper, which can be cut out and

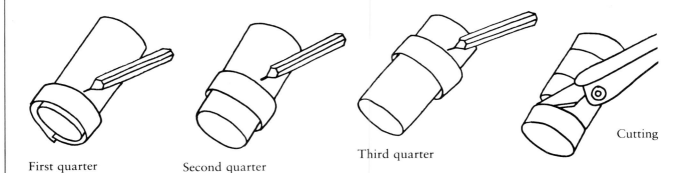

First quarter   Second quarter   Third quarter   Cutting

wrapped round the roll to act as a measure. Starting at one end of the toilet roll middle, wrap the paper round and draw a line on the cardboard, marking one quarter of the way up. Slide the paper along and mark the half-way stage (right round the roll), and slide again to mark the third quarter. Follow each line carefully with the knife, ensuring that the cardboard is not damaged too much by pressing inwards. If some rolls start to come apart, they can either be discarded or a spot of glue used to repair them. They will all be covered, eventually, and the cold-water paste will bond them.

3. Cold-water paste

Use a cold-water paste powder or wallpaper paste *only*. Any other type of adhesive is far too strong and 'sticky' for papier mâché work. Even the clear liquid glue, obtainable in 5-litre containers, which many schools use, is far too messy for this type of work. Cold-water paste can be mixed to any consistency but it is advisable to mix it in the proportion that would be used for hanging wallpaper. It will probably thicken as the session progresses and, if this happens, can be thinned out slightly by adding a little water and mixing well.

If the design is to be painted directly on to the completed ring without being drawn on first, there is no need to wait until the paste has dried before applying the paint. In fact, a very pleasing effect can be obtained by painting while the paste is still in a liquid state as the colours will seep into one another and create an 'Impressionist mood'. It is suggested in Section 7 that the paint be mixed with a PVA medium; this is both to thicken the paint and to give it a reasonable amount of resistance to the varnish before the colours run into one another. Painting directly on to wet paste will also add to this resistance.

4. Brushes

There are many methods of papier mâché work and, when thinking of this type of craft, most people imagine a bucket of paste and paper which is applied, by hand, to a wire-frame skeleton. This is, indeed, an effective way of creating three-dimensional models but, for papier mâché which requires a particular shape to be followed, application by brush is ideal. It is a much neater way of working and creates less general mess. It also means that there is more control over the group and a larger number of students can be accommodated at any one time.

Because the medium is a water-based paste, any type of brush may be used and, providing that it is washed thoroughly afterwards, a paintbrush should suffer no ill effects from being used in cold-water paste. It is always as well for the organiser to check the brushes after the session and not just rely on the student's idea of washing up!

Fingers can be kept relatively clean by encouraging the students to let the brush do all the work. The newspaper and white-paper pieces are very easily picked up, individually, by a brushful of paste and will come away from the pile of pieces, one at a time, if very light pressure is applied.

5. Newspaper and white paper

There is a very important and logical reason for using two different colours of paper. This is, simply, so that students can tell how far round the ring they have worked. This ensures that the whole ring is worked evenly, inside and out, and avoids the possibility of working twice over one section at the expense of the next. Ending with a white layer ensures a neutral base colour to which to apply the paint, whatever shade may be chosen.

Newspaper is excellent for this type of work as it absorbs the paste very quickly and bonds tightly when it is dry.

If it is not possible to obtain white newsprint, which is the same quality as newspaper, there are two alternatives. Select an absorbent white paper which is fairly thin so that the paste will seep through it quickly or, better still, tear off the white edges of the newspaper, as this will ensure the same quality throughout.

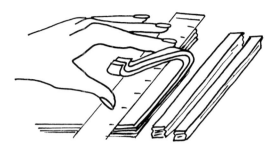

From the diagram of the work area it will be seen that two boxes of paper strips are suggested and, although this may take time in preparation, it is probably quicker and less of a fuss for the organiser to have these strips ready than it would be for students to contend with large sheets of newspaper in a limited work space. Use a ruler as a tearing guide and remove the white edges of the paper. Keep these white strips in a box.

The same method can be used to tear off the strips of newspaper. It may be possible to tear a whole newspaper at a time – certainly half should be possible. Keep moving the ruler back 1 cm after each tear and place the newspaper strips in a separate box.

The strips do not need to be exactly 1 cm in width, this is just a rough guide, but the smaller the squares, the more manageable they will be and the more solid the finished ring. It *is*, however, most important that the paper be *torn* and not cut with scissors. Tearing newspaper leaves a frayed edge into which the paste can seep. This makes for a smooth bonding and flat finish. If the newspaper is cut the edges are definite and will remain so, even when the paper is pasted and dry.

The length of the strips is not important as they will, eventually, be torn into squares. Students can then take a few strips at a time from the box and make their own individual pile of squares from which to work.

6. Paper towels

These are a very useful item to have to hand, both for the pasting stage and for painting, later on. If towels are too expensive or difficult to come by, a small sheet of newspaper for each child will cut down the amount of paste and paint on the work surface.

7. Paint

Use a ready-mix or powder paint and add a small amount of PVA medium. This will help to 'set' the paint and give it a certain amount of resistance to the varnish so that the colours do not immediately run into one another. Mix the paint and glue in clean margarine tubs, with lids (the colour can be marked on the lid of each tub). This will facilitate storage of the paint for a future session. If paint is stored, stir it well before the next use as separation may have occurred.

| | Greetings Card Baubles

Here's an interesting way of using up last year's
Christmas cards or saving those special birthday or
anniversary greetings which you just can't throw away.
Made up into these baubles they will be useful as well as
decorative.

METHOD   (Bauble I)

I. Trace the circle and the equilateral triangle at the end of this
chapter. Stick them to a piece of card and cut them out to use as
templates.

2. Draw circles on the greetings cards to include those parts of the
pictures which you wish to keep. Cut them out carefully. You will
need 20 discs in all.

3. Using the template of the triangle, place it in the centre of a disc so that all three points touch the perimeter of the circle.

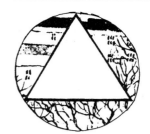

4. Holding the work firmly, fold the three 'wings' over the triangle so that they encase it. Run your fingers down each side to make a sharp crease.

5. Unfold the 'wings', remove the triangle and repeat the process with the other 19 discs.

6. Count them out into four groups of five and work on the first group as follows.

Group 1   Group 2   Group 3   Group 4

7. Arrange them on the work surface so that the top points come together at the centre of a flower shape.

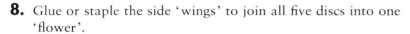

8. Glue or staple the side 'wings' to join all five discs into one 'flower'.

glue

NB: It is more important that the straight sides of the triangle fit snugly than to have the tops of the wings fitting on the outside (these can always be trimmed later, if necessary) so keep checking inside the shape that all the edges lie side by side.

glue

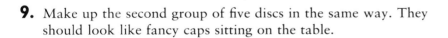

9. Make up the second group of five discs in the same way. They should look like fancy caps sitting on the table.

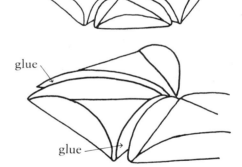

10. Go back to the first 'cap' that you made. You will notice that there are five spare 'wings' around the bottom.

To each of these 'wings' glue or staple one of the shapes from your third group of five discs.

11. Do the same with the remaining 'cap' and your last group of five discs.

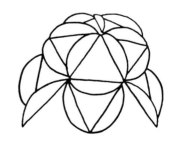

12. To fit the two shapes together, hold one 'cap' downwards and the other 'cap' upwards. You will see that the five pieces round each one will slide into one another, like the cogs of a wheel.

Glue or staple them in to position *except for the last 'wing'*.

13. Before making the whole shape solid by fixing the last piece, take a small offcut of card and roll it tightly. Tie it firmly round the centre with thread and leave a long end for hanging the decoration.

14. Place the roll of card inside the shape with the thread hanging out and glue or staple the last two 'wings' together.

NB: If you want the thread to come out at a different place, remember to insert it in position before fixing the particular 'wings' concerned.

15. When the shape is dry it can be hung up, either as a Christmas-tree decoration or, if you have made a larger bauble, suspended amongst the paper-chains and trimmings.

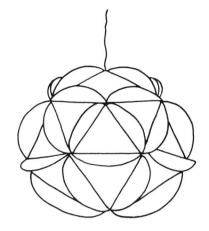

METHOD   (Bauble 2)

1. Trace the square at the end of this chapter. Stick it to card and cut it out to use as a template.

2. Draw squares on the greetings cards to include those parts of the pictures which you wish to keep. Cut them out carefully. You will need six squares for each bauble.

3. Take one square, picture uppermost, and fold it diagonally, corner to corner. Make sure the sides are together and that one corner is lying directly on the other. Accuracy at this stage will mean that your bauble will fit well when you glue it together.

4. Open it out and fold it diagonally to the other corner.

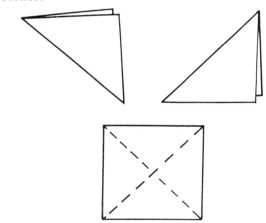

5. Turn the card face downwards and fold it in half to make a rectangle.

6. Open the card, turn it and fold to the other corners to make the second rectangle.

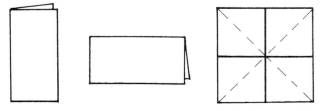

7. Do the same to the other five cards and stand them on the table so that they look like small rocket ships ready to take off!

8. Put two 'rockets' to one side. These will eventually form the top and bottom of the bauble, so you can choose your best pictures for these. You now have a group of four left.

9. Take two 'rockets' from the group of four. Flatten them gently and glue one quarter of the first one on to the top of one quarter of the second one, as in the diagram. Make sure that the pictures face *upwards*.

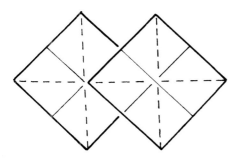

10. Glue the third and fourth 'rockets' to the first two, in the same way (one quarter overlapping) so that you have a line of four.

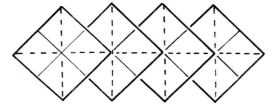

11. To join up the circle, glue the first quarter of the first 'rocket' to the last quarter of the fourth 'rocket', as in the diagram.

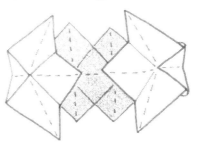

12. Choose one of the remaining two 'rockets' to be the bottom and glue the underside of the card. Attach it to the ring of rockets so that it seals all the loose points which are hanging down.

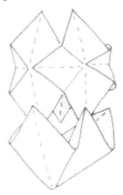

13. Before gluing the top into place, make a roll of card, tied round with thread and insert the card into the shape with the thread hanging out. This will enable the bauble to be hung.

14. Glue the top on to the shape in the same way as you sealed the bottom.

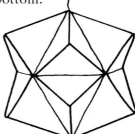

Small baubles can be used for Christmas-tree decorations and larger ones suspended amongst the paper chains and trimmings.

ORGANISING YOUR MATERIALS

I. Setting up the work area

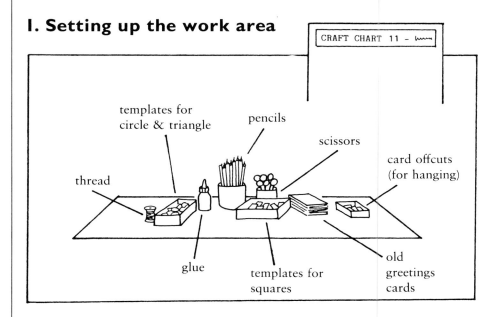

CRAFT CHART 11 –

templates for circle & triangle

pencils

scissors

card offcuts (for hanging)

thread

glue

templates for squares

old greetings cards

The amount of equipment placed on the work area depends on the amount of preparation the organiser feels ought to be done. If the children are young, it is advisable to prepare all the templates, but if the students are to make their own templates, card, rulers and compasses will need to be provided as well.

2. Old greetings cards

These can be collected in January and kept in store until the end of the year. Alternatively, ask children to bring in their own selection at the time of the session. Some children are unreliable in this respect, so have plently of spare cards available. The number of cards required will depend on the size of the circle/square being used and, to a certain extent, the type of picture on each card.

An interesting variation is to use plain, manila card instead of greetings cards. The circles/squares can be painted before being put together or made up first and then decorated with coloured sticky papers or glitter.

3. Templates
(a) Circle and triangle
The circle and triangle which can be found at the end of this chapter may be traced and used as templates for Bauble 1. Any size of circle can be used and, as a rough guide, the width of the completed solid will be just under double the diameter of the circle used: e.g. a circle of 6.5 cm diameter will give a solid 12 cm across.

As the discs need to fit together exactly to give a neat and polished finish to the work, it is *most important* that the triangle is the correct

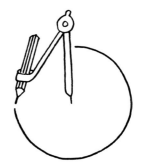

equilateral triangle for the circle. To make this it will be necessary to use a pair of compasses and not just trust to a ruler and the eye.

To make your own templates, choose the radius of the circle required and describe (draw) the circle with the compasses. Put this to one side as the pattern for the circle.

With *exactly the same radius*, describe another circle. Place the point of the compasses anywhere on the circumference and describe two small arcs which cut the circumference at each side. *Keeping the same radius*, move the point of the compasses to each of these intersections in turn and describe the arcs which cut the circle. Continue round the circle until it has been cut six times – it should work out exactly. This is the method for drawing hexagons (six-sided figures), but as a triangle only requires three sides and three points, take alternate arcs and join them using a ruler and pencil.

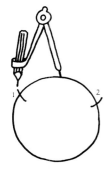
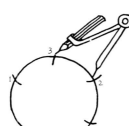
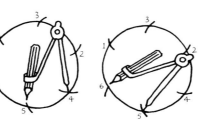
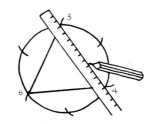

The drawings can then be 'rough' cut, stuck to card and used for drawing round to make as many templates as necessary.

NB: When preparing the compasses for use, always ensure that the tip of the pencil is flush with the metal point when the compasses are closed (stand them upright on the work surface to check). This is necessary for accuracy in the drawing.

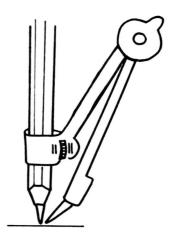

Another important point to remember when folding the 'wings' over the sides of the triangle, is to ensure that the points of the triangle come right to the edge of the circle at all three places. If this is not done accurately the errors will be magnified as more pieces are fitted together, and the finished shape will look lop-sided.

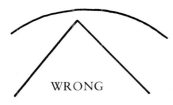
WRONG

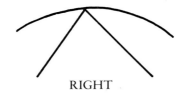
RIGHT

(b) Squares

Use the square at the end of this chapter to make templates for Bauble 2.

This solid shape uses some of the basic principles of the Japanese art of Origami. There are two folds used in Bauble 2, the *valley fold* which points downwards (like a valley) and the *mountain fold* which points upwards (like a mountain).

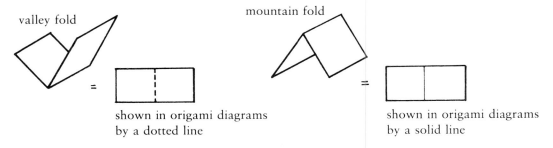

valley fold

= shown in origami diagrams by a dotted line

mountain fold

= shown in origami diagrams by a solid line

When seen from the picture side of the greetings card, the diagonal folds should be valley folds and the those running from top to bottom and side to side should be mountain folds.

A rough guide to the size of the finished solid can be obtained by remembering that the size of the square used will be approximately that of the finished bauble: i.e. 5 cm squares will produce a solid 5 cm across.

4. Glue

Although a PVA adhesive is recommended because it will dry to a transparent finish, it should be spread quite thinly to prevent 'oozing' from between the cards. Children can use glue spreaders or offcuts of card to apply the glue or, if using a nozzled pot, encourage them to hold the nozzle right down on to the card so that only a thin line of glue is squeezed out. It is only necessary to glue round the edges of each section.

It is possible to insert fingers inside Bauble 2 when gluing the bottom section in place but a reasonable amount of glue should be applied to the last section in order to fix it securely.

5. Thread

For very small baubles which need a delicate finish, fine fishing-line is recommended. Normal dressmakers' cotton is really not strong enough for the weight that has to be carried. For more robust solids, use an embroidery thread or thin butchers' string.

FURTHER SUGGESTIONS

Both these solid shapes will roll and could be decorated with numbers on each face to act as dice. Bauble 1 will give range from 1 to 20 (as there are 20 faces) and Bauble 2 will provide 1 to 12 (there are 12 faces on this solid).

Although the second shape would appear to be easier – there are fewer pieces to deal with and the finished effect does not look too complicated – don't be deceived. Some children will find the instruction to stick four shapes in a line very confusing, so be prepared for some peculiar-looking designs!

It is recommended that the organiser tries both Baubles before attempting a craft session. This has two advantages. It not only gives first-hand experience of any pitfalls that might occur but also gives a model of each for the children to work by and aim towards.

TEMPLATES FOR BAUBLES

BAUBLE 1

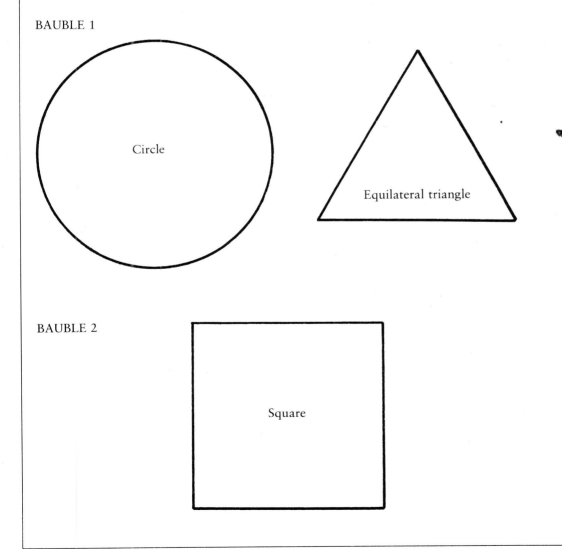

Circle

Equilateral triangle

BAUBLE 2

Square

12 Space Game

Although the instructions here lead to a Times Table Game, the principle can be used for any subject where a competitive element is required – from spelling bees to Scout/Guide badges.

METHOD (The Planets)

This work teaches the technique of using a drawing pin, string and pencil as a pair of compasses to draw large circles (representing the planets) on the coloured craft paper. Scale is unimportant, but try to keep the sizes accurate in relation to each other – i.e. Jupiter the largest, Pluto and Mercury the smallest, etc. (see later pages for details).

1. Tie a small loop in one end of the string. Push the drawing pin through the loop. This is the point of your compasses.

2. Select the length of radius required (half the width of your planet) and tie the string to the pencil at that place.

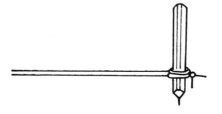

3. Push the drawing pin firmly into the sugar paper at the correct place and, keeping the string taut and the pencil upright, draw the circle with the pencil. (You may need help to hold the drawing pin in place if the circle is very large.)

4. Repeat the process, using different coloured paper for each planet and adjusting the length of the string as necessary.

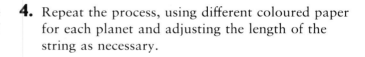
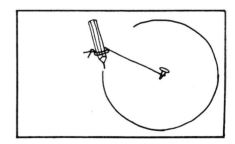

5. To make the sun, use yellow paper and draw a narrow segment only. The sun is so much larger than all the other planets that a representation is all that is needed. Draw lots of flames onto red paper to fix to the sun's edge.

6. Draw small circles next to the planets which have natural satellites – 2 for Mars, 13 for Jupiter, etc.

Outline all the planets and flames with a black felt pen *before* cutting them out.

7. Write the name on each planet in large black letters, and the other information required (see p. 86).

8. Cut strips of white paper to act as 'paths' running from planet to planet.

9. Edge these 'paths' with a red line (use a metre rule to keep the lines straight) and write the required information along each strip.

The length of the 'paths' can be shortened or added to when the game is mounted on the wall or ceiling.

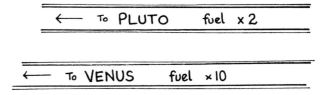

METHOD (The Rockets)

1. Take the four pattern pieces for the rocket (which can be found at the end of this chapter) and transfer them to card. Cut them out.

2. Glue the body of the rocket to a piece of foil, metallic paper or lurex.

3. Glue the three 'engines' to a different coloured piece of foil/paper, etc. (sweet wrappers are large enough for this).

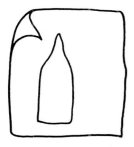 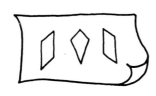

4. When the glue is dry, cut out all four pieces.

5. Glue the top section of the 'engines' to the base of the body, as in the diagram.

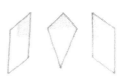

Apply glue to back of shaded areas only

6. Fix a drawing pin through the centre of the rocket's body and cover the pin's head by gluing a named label across it.

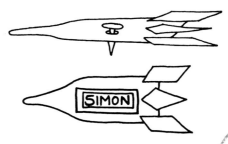

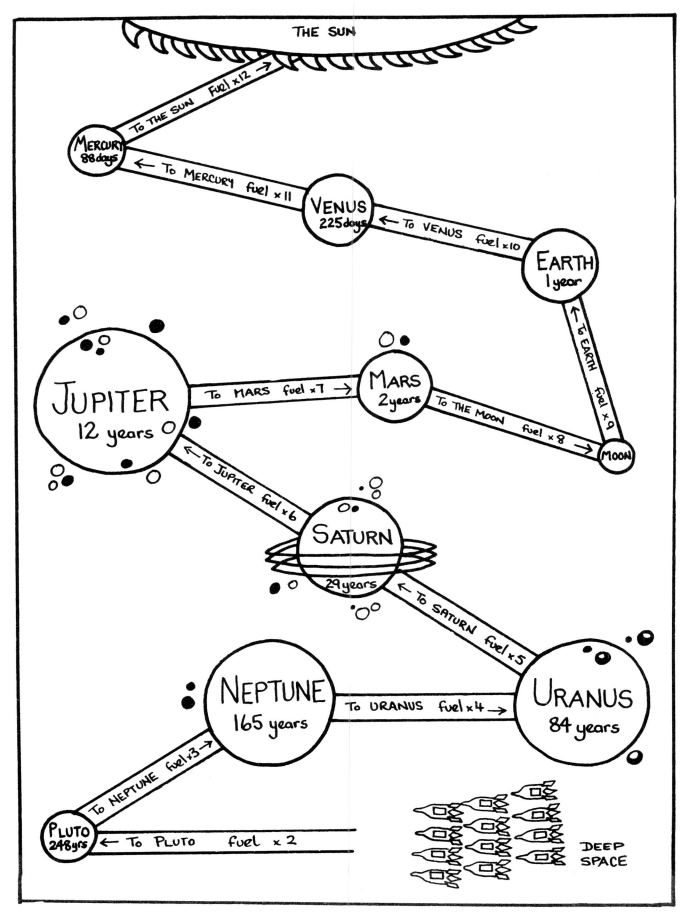

THE SUN

To THE SUN   fuel × 12 →

MERCURY
88 days

← To MERCURY   fuel × 11

VENUS
225 days

← To VENUS   fuel × 10

EARTH
1 year

↑ To EARTH   fuel × 9

JUPITER
12 years

To MARS   fuel × 7 →

MARS
2 years

To THE MOON   fuel × 8 →

MOON

← To JUPITER   fuel × 6

SATURN
29 years

← To SATURN   fuel × 5

NEPTUNE
165 years

To URANUS   fuel × 4 →

URANUS
84 years

To NEPTUNE   fuel × 3 →

PLUTO
248 yrs

← To PLUTO   fuel × 2

DEEP
SPACE

PLAYING THE GAME

The game is designed to give a visual representation of each child's success at learning his multiplication tables. All the rockets start in *Deep Space*, and each child 'fuels' his or her space craft by learning the designated times table, thus moving on to the next planet: the object is to arrive, eventually, on the Sun. Obviously teachers will have their own methods of testing tables, whether by weekly written tests, setting aside a few minutes each morning for class and individual oral work, or both. Whatever method is preferred, the teacher should be satisfied that the child is completely conversant with the table before allowing the rocket to be moved.

ORGANISING YOUR MATERIALS

I. Setting up the work area

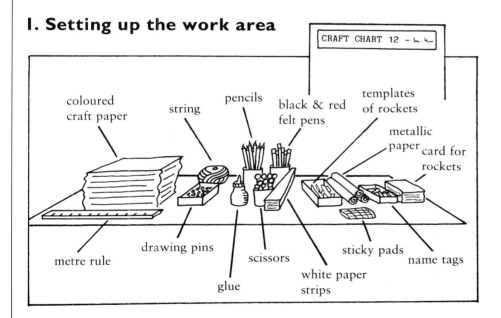

CRAFT CHART 12 – ᴧ ᴧ

Set up a 'stock' table of materials to which students can go to collect the materials as and when required. Many of them will be handling large sheets of sugar paper so they may prefer to work on the floor to draw out the circles. Protect the flooring from drawing-pin marks by providing a small square of fairly thick card to place under the sugar paper where the drawing pin goes through. Although this will cause a slight 'lump' in the middle of the paper while the circle is being drawn, it will make no difference to the accuracy of drawing.

2. Organising the group work

Make a list of all the individual jobs to be done and divide up your group so that each element is covered. Remember that the bigger planets will need at least two pairs of hands. Instead of writing directly on to each planet, one student could be given the task of writing large named labels to fix to the appropriate circle and another could write labels for the orbital information. These can be checked for neatness and accuracy before being fixed to each planet, lessening the chance of spoiling someone else's work.

Having looked at the plan of the game, decide how much of it you require for your purpose. For example, multiplication tables between 2 and 12 (inclusive) can be accommodated between the planets if the rockets begin in Deep Space and use the Moon as one of the landing stages. This can be reduced to ×10 if the spaceships start on Pluto and go straight from Mars to Earth, missing out the Moon. Use the following check-list to ensure that all the work which needs to be done has been allocated.

Elements of work to be covered

Drawing, outlining and cutting the Sun.
Drawing, outlining and cutting the flames.
Drawing, outlining and cutting Mercury.
Drawing, outlining and cutting Venus.
Drawing, outlining and cutting Earth.
Drawing, outlining and cutting the Moon.
Drawing, outlining and cutting Mars plus 2 satellites.
Drawing, outlining and cutting Jupiter plus 13 satellites.
Drawing, outlining and cutting Saturn plus 10 satellites.
Drawing, outlining and cutting the 3 rings of Saturn.
Drawing, outlining and cutting Uranus plus 5 satellites.
Drawing, outlining and cutting Neptune plus 2 satellites.
Drawing, outlining and cutting Pluto.
Name labels for all planets plus Deep Space.
Orbital information for all planets.
Directions on white paper 'paths'.

Individual rockets.

When each group has finished its task, the children can then proceed with their own, individual rockets.

3. Coloured craft paper

Multi-coloured craft paper is available in an assortment of bright colours, up to A3 size. However, any type of coloured paper will be suitable and sticky pads can be used to fix the planets to the wall or ceiling. The size of the planets will obviously depend on the amount of space available for the overall display.

4. Templates of rockets

Prepare a few templates from card which the students can draw round to make their own rockets. Patterns for the body and engines of the space craft can be found at the end of this chapter.

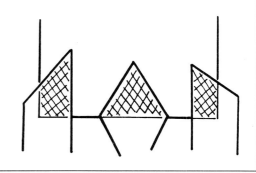

When fixing the completed engines to the body of the rocket, ensure that only a small dab of glue is used on the shaded areas, as these are the only places where the parts join.

5. Metallic paper

Many educational suppliers carry a stock of rolls of metallic paper in an assortment of colours. Domestic kitchen foil can also be used for the body of the rocket but it is suggested that, as foil is often difficult to cut, it is best to fold the foil over the edges of the rocket to make a neat shape. Foil wrappers for chocolates, which are often printed in colourful designs, are an ideal alternative for covering the 'engines'.

6. White strips

Having decided on the overall size of the game, it is advisable to prepare these strips in advance. They can be cut, using a guillotine or craft knife, from white newsprint so that they are ready to give to the students for the information to be written on. Have plenty of 'spares' to hand so that the paths between the planets can be lengthened if necessary.

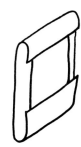

7. Name tags

Cut pieces of white card to a size suitable for the centre of the rockets. Each child should write his or her name clearly and a border pattern can be coloured before fixing the card to the rocket, over the drawing-pin head.

8. Display area

If the room has a low ceiling, this is an ideal place for the game to be mounted. It keeps it out of the way and utilises space which would probably not be used otherwise. The game will need to be displayed for some time, so choose a place where it will not be disturbed while in use.

TEMPLATES OF ROCKET

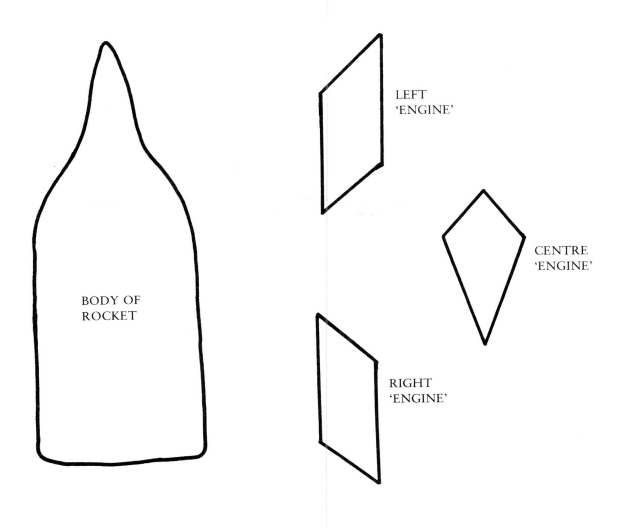

BODY OF
ROCKET

LEFT
'ENGINE'

CENTRE
'ENGINE'

RIGHT
'ENGINE'

TABLE OF INFORMATION

Name of planet	Time taken to orbit Sun	Number of natural satellites	Suggested radius
Mercury	88 days	0	12 cm
Venus	225 days	0	15 cm
Earth	1 year	1	15 cm
Mars	2 years	2	15 cm
Jupiter	12 years	13	35 cm
Saturn	29 years	3 rings and 10 satellites	26 cm
Uranus	84 years	5	30 cm
Neptune	165 years	2	30 cm
Pluto	248 years	0	10 cm

13 Collage

This charming little bee can be made up into a picture in its own right or mass-produced by a group to form a classroom frieze. Add flowers or a beehive to the picture to give a focal point.

METHOD

1. Cut a piece of background card on to which to mount your picture.

Cut a piece of blue material to fit the card.

2. Glue around the edge of the card and stick the blue material in place.

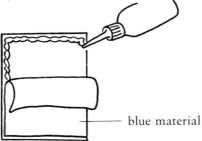

blue material

3. Trace the patterns at the end of this chapter and number each piece, as shown.

4. Cut each piece out from the appropriate coloured material.

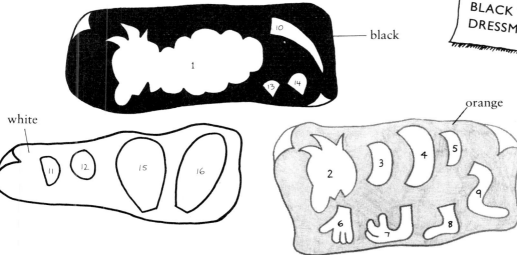

black

white

orange

5. Without gluing, lay the pieces on the background, building up the picture and making sure that the bee is in the right place.

6. Start with the black body piece (number 1) and glue around the edge of this shape. Stick it in position on the background board.

7. Glue around the orange head piece (number 2) and glue that in position. The black shape which is already there will show you exactly where to position the head.

8. Glue the three orange bands for the body (numbers 3, 4 and 5) and stick these in place to form the bee's striped body.

9. Numbers 6 and 7 are the bee's hands, so fix these into position, as illustrated.

10. Do the same with the legs (numbers 8 and 9).

11. The black piece (number 10) is the sting. Glue this in place, pointing downwards.

12. The small pieces 11, 12, 13 and 14 make up the eyes. Glue the two black shapes (11 and 12) on to the lower halves of the white pieces (13 and 14). They should fit exactly.

Then lay the eyes on the bee's face and, when you are satisfied that they are in the right position, glue them into place.

13. Glue around the edges of the wings, sticking number 15 in place first, so that it sits behind number 16. If the material is firm (or if using coloured paper for the collage instead of fabric) the wings can be pleated, glued at the bottoms only and left free at the tops to give a more three-dimensional effect.

14. Using a glue pot with a nozzle which will administer only a narrow line of glue, work round the outside of each piece, outlining with the black wool.

Work on a small section at a time, gluing and patting the wool into place. Use dressmaking pins to hold awkward corners in position until dry. Outlining all the pieces will bring the bee to 'life'.

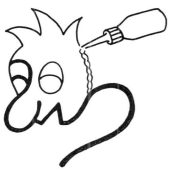

15. Complete your picture by gluing a frame around it. See Chapter 5 for suggestions on framing.

ORGANISING YOUR MATERIALS

I. Setting up the work area

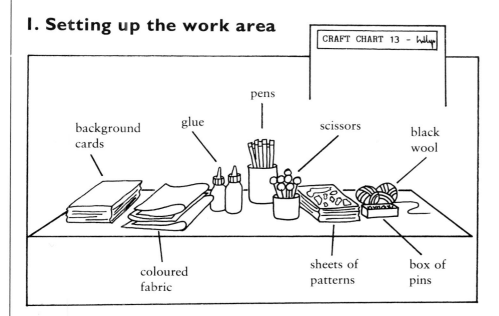

Decide whether students will be making individual collages or working as a group to produce a combined picture or frieze.

2. Card (for backgrounds)

(a) Individual pictures
Choose a fairly thick card which will be suitable for the background. If all the pictures are to be the same size, the card can be guillotined beforehand and presented at the session, ready cut for use. This prevents wastage and ensures that there is enough to go round.

(b) Frieze
Background card is unnecessary and the bees can be built up on the large pattern piece (1). The hand (6), leg (8) and sting (10) can be fixed just under the edge of the large body piece.

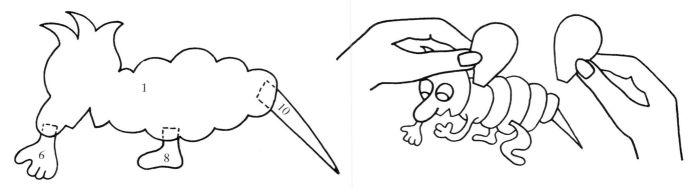

The wings can be edged separately, with the black wool, and fixed into position on the body when the bee has been mounted on the frieze.

Instead of card, prepare a length of background paper for the frieze or cover a display board. Add flowers so that the bees can be displayed on and around them. Students may wish to make their own flowers as well.

Alternatively, mark out a space for a beehive, which can be made in advance and kept to one side. When all the bees have been fixed to the frieze, produce the beehive – as a surprise – to add the finishing touch.

To give a more realistic effect, photocopy the bee patterns in two or three different sizes so that an element of perspective is obtained. Display the larger bees at the bottom of the work and the smaller ones towards the top so that they appear to be flying home from a distance.

3. Coloured material

Any type of fabric may be used. A bonded material, such as felt, is best for young children as it will not fray when cut. However, most fabrics will survive if handled with a reasonable amount of respect once cut into shape. Any edge which shows signs of fraying can be stuck carefully and will eventually be covered with the black wool.

An excellent craft paper called 'Vivelle' is obtainable from most educational suppliers. This is a flocked paper which gives the appearance of being a felt-type fabric but which has a paper backing. It is obtainable in packets of various sizes and assorted colours. Many craft shops will also stock this type of flocked paper. The pattern pieces can be drawn round directly on to the paper backing so that no pen marks show when the work is displayed.

NB: If drawing out bees on the *back* of any materials, make sure that the students reverse the pattern pieces before drawing and cutting out. (To make up bees which face the other way, reverse the patterns deliberately.)

For younger children, these bees can be drawn and cut from coloured paper rather than fabric. Instead of using wool to outline the sections, allow the glue to dry and then draw around all the outlines with a black felt pen to make the colours stand out.

4. Glue

Use a white PVA glue, which dries to a transparent finish. A narrow line of glue around the edge of each piece is all that is required.

A pot with a nozzle will give maximum control over the amount of glue being applied. A spreader can be very messy when using fabric and will only add to the chances of the material's fraying before it can be stuck into place.

When sticking large areas of fabric (i.e. the background or the body) lay the piece in position first 'dry', and lift half of the shape to apply the glue. When the first half has stuck down, lift the second half and glue in place. In this way the student does not have a piece of very sticky material hanging in mid-air, wondering where to place it.

PVA adhesive, applied around the edges of the sections by a nozzled glue pot, is ideal for fixing the wool in place. As it is transparent when dry, any over-enthusiastic squirt of glue will not look quite as untidy once the work has completely 'set'.

5. Patterns

Reproduce the pattern pieces at the end of this chapter and present them to the students in one of the following ways:

(a) *as a complete sheet*

Pin pattern to fabric and cut out.

Draw round shape on to material.

Use carbon paper to transfer shapes to the material.

(b) *as templates*

Make templates from card which the students can draw round on to the appropriate coloured material.

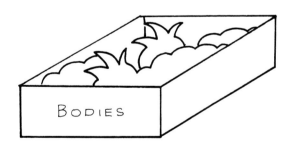

6. Wool

Use an oddment of black wool for outlining all the sections in your collage. This will bring the colours to life and make the work show up well from a distance. The thickness of the wool will depend on the size of your picture. If you consider that 4-ply wool is too heavy for your work, take the strands apart and use one or two strands only. If the wool will not stay in place around awkward corners, use pins, pushed into the background material, to hold the wool until the glue has dried. Remove these pins with a twisting movement or you may pull the edging away from the picture.

TEMPLATES FOR BEE

14 Candlemaking

Here is an introduction to candlemaking which will cost almost nothing. These candles are quick to make and a good stall filler for bazaars and fairs. They are very effective as table centres for dinner parties.

METHOD

1. Remove one candle from the packet and put it to one side. Break up all the other candles, removing the wicks, and place them in the clean baked-bean tin.

3. Place the whole contraption on the heat to boil the water, and keep at a low simmer so that the wax melts in the tin.

2. Stand the tin in the old saucepan into which you have poured water.

4. Add the stub of coloured wax crayon and mix well, using the old knife.

5. While the wax is melting, seat the kitchen funnel in the jam-jar and fill the jar with enough cold water to block off the spout of the funnel.

6. Take the single candle which you removed from the packet and use the knife to trim off some of the wax from the top so that more wick shows. Hold the candle with its wick poking into the kitchen funnel and measure the length required to the top of the funnel. Cut through the wax with the knife and through the wick with the scissors.

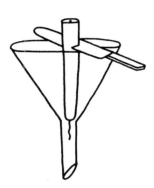

7. When the wax has melted, stir well. Hold the centre candle in position – wick down into the spout – and pour a little of the wax into the funnel so that the candle is held in place. Leave to set for a little while.

8. Place the ice-cubes in a polythene bag and hit each one, gently, with the hammer to break it in half.

9. Arrange the ice-cubes around the inside of the funnel, standing them on each other's 'shoulders', keeping them away from the central candle as much as possible.

10. Give the melted wax a good stir and pour it into the funnel, over the ice-cubes and to cover the white candle completely.

Leave to set (approximately two hours).

11. Unmould the candle over the bowl – remember that what were once ice-cubes will now be water; you may get wet feet otherwise!

ORGANISING YOUR MATERIALS

I. Setting up the work area

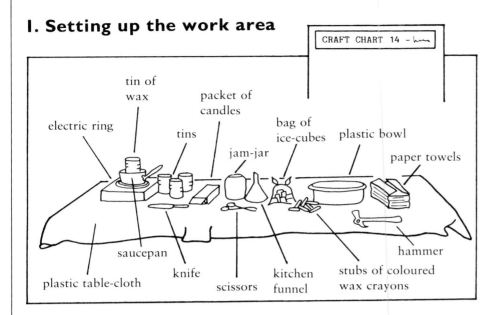

CRAFT CHART 14 –

Choose a sturdy table on which to set out the equipment. It is most important that the candles are left to harden on a surface which is out of the way so that they will not be knocked over accidentally. This may mean providing a second table, set to one side.

This piece of craftwork is not recommended for large groups but can be offered as one of a number of craft projects, especially if ancillary help is available and an adult oversees the whole session from start to finish. Five or six students should be able to complete the work in an afternoon or evening session.

Safety precautions: if using an electric ring, ensure that the flex is safely stowed and there is no chance of anyone tripping over it and spilling hot water and wax. Although wax melts at a low temperature and will not actually burn the skin, it can be quite painful if spilt on hands and arms.

Do not allow the wax (either in melted or solid form) anywhere near a sink or drain. Use the plastic bowl for any water or washing up required and empty it afterwards on to the flower beds. Melted wax might look harmless but will cause problems with the drainage if tipped away down a sink.

2. Plastic table-cloth

Candlemaking can make quite a mess and it is advisable to protect the work surface, not only from spillage of melted wax but also from the small pieces

of wax and wick which will inevitably be strewn around. Using newspaper or cotton cloths will not do the job as well, as both are absorbent and melted wax will just seep through the fibres and stick to the table. If a plastic table-cloth is not available, a number of plastic carrier bags, split open and overlapped, can be placed under newspaper to give this protection.

3. Electric ring/primus stove/cooker

Any source of heat may be used but do be aware of the safety aspect when preparing this type of craftwork.

Always clean the electric ring (or cooker) before it cools down. No matter how carefully organised the session might be, small droplets of water containing wax will splash over the heater during use. These are easily wiped off with paper towels after the heater has been turned off and disconnected. Reheat the cooker before cleaning if it has been allowed to cool too much to clean easily. Trying to scrape off wax after it has set will mark and damage the heater.

Be especially aware of safety if using a gas appliance.

4. Tins

Make a collection of tins – large fruit tins, baked bean tins, tins from beer making kits – as these are ideal for containing melting wax. They can be squeezed at the top to make a pouring lip and are easily handled with a piece of kitchen or paper towel.

Use a separate tin for each colour required. The tin can be topped up with the same colour when necessary. After the session, allow any coloured wax to set in its tin as this can be stored intact when cold and used again later.

5. Saucepan

The very nature of candle wax is to burn. For this reason it is essential to keep it away from direct heat or naked flames. Working on the principle that water and wax do not mix, stand the tin in an old saucepan of water, which will fulfil two purposes. Firstly, the water acts as a barrier, keeping the wax away from the source of heat, and secondly it will be the hot water that melts the wax as opposed to the flame or electric ring itself. Make sure it is an old saucepan as it will become waxy and unsuitable for vegetables! Clean it after use by taking it outside with a kettle of hot water and rinsing it over the flower bed. Do not wash it up in the kitchen sink!!

6. Wax

Packets of wax granules can be purchased from most craft shops and educational suppliers but these are only useful, really, if a lot of candlemaking is intended. For a 'one-off' experiment or for trying out the craft at home, it is far less expensive to use a packet of household candles. Using one of the candles as the central stem for the new candle dispenses with the need for a separate wick.

Break each candle along its length and pull the wax off the wick before putting the pieces into the tin. If some wick does find its way into the tin, this can be retrieved with the knife once the wax has melted. Candle wax melts at a very low temperature, so bring the water to the boil and then lower the heat to keep the water at a gentle simmer.

7. Coloured wax crayons

Dyes for colouring candle wax can be purchased in liquid or powder form from many craft shops but the cheapest way of colouring is to use old stubs of wax crayons which can be dropped into the tin and melted along with the white candles. Use the knife to mix the colour into the wax. Please note that some modern crayons, especially the chubby ones, have an ingredient which prevents melting, so these are not suitable for this work. Different colours can be produced by adding two different coloured crayons to a tin and blending them together as they melt. Note that the colour produced in the tin will be darker than the finished colour; the shade will lighten as the wax sets. If a deep colour is required, more crayon must be added to the melted wax. Use a separate tin for each colour.

8. Knife

Use an old knife, not one from the best cutlery set. Keep a paper towel handy to wipe the knife each time it has been used in the wax. It is much easier to keep it clean if wiped when warm and, in this way, one knife can be used in a number of tins without detriment to the colours.

9. Kitchen funnel

Choosing a mould

Many ordinary, everyday utensils can be used as moulds for candlemaking without the need for expensive equipment. When choosing a mould it is important to look at the diameter of the container, as this will dictate the thickness of the wick which should be used. If the wick is too thick for the candle, there will not be enough wax to feed it and it will keep going out. If the wick is too small for the diameter of the finished candle, there will be too much melted wax created and the wick will drown. Therefore, when using a white, household candle as the centre stem, it is important to choose a mould which will not add too much wax to the existing candle or the result will be disappointing.

The funnel

A kitchen funnel is ideal for this purpose. Not only is it an interesting shape but candles made in a funnel do not take too long to set. It is a mould which will produce a decorative candle using a household candle at its centre and, as it is tapered, the volume of wax will not be too great for the thin wick to cope with. In this particular 'lace' design, the candlelight will shine through the holes, the melted wax will spill through the openings like a miniature volcano and the candle will, eventually, burn down completely. Of course, any wax remaining when the candle has been used can be cleaned, broken up and put back in the melting pot and used for the next candle.

There is no need to treat the funnel with any lubricant before filling it. Just make sure that it is clean. Do this by taking the funnel outside with a kettle of hot water, and pour the water through the funnel (right up the sides and over the rim – mind your fingers!) so that it runs out through the spout. Do this over the flower bed. It is best to clean the funnel immediately after use rather than leave it until the next time it is needed.

To unmould the candle, hold the funnel in both hands and work round the rim, releasing the candle. Do not use an implement; gentle pressure is all that is required. Then turn the funnel, spout up, and shake it gently to release the candle. *Do this over a bowl* – remember, what were ice cubes will now be water.

If the funnel is very large there is no need to fill it completely, as this will use a lot of wax. The height of the candle will depend on the length of the central stem, which should just be covered with the coloured wax. The edge of the base can be neatened when the candle has been unmoulded.

10. Jam-jar

The purpose of using a jam-jar is twofold. It is a convenient way of supporting the mould while the candle is setting and, being see-through, it enables the candlemaker to gauge accurately the amount of cold water needed to block off the spout of the kitchen funnel. Choose a reasonably heavy jar to give maximum stability.

When pouring the first centimetre of wax into the funnel to set the centre candle, pour very gently so that the water will prevent the wax from entering the spout. It can be quite difficult to unmould the candle if the wax extends into the spout of the funnel.

11. Ice-cubes

These can be made well in advance and one tray of ice-cubes is ample for one, probably two, candles. Protect them from melting before use by putting them in a plastic bag and wrapping them in lots of sheets of newspaper. This acts as insulation and should keep them frozen until required.

Do not break them up too much. The 'lace' effect of the finished candle is much better if the holes are large, and the ice-cubes will not melt quite as quickly if they are big. The stage of putting the ice-cubes into the funnel and arranging them around the sides must be done quickly, especially if the room is warm. They will begin to melt immediately and, if the wax is not poured on them very soon, a pool of water will appear at the base of the cubes. As wax will not mix with water, this pool will prevent the majority of the coloured wax from joining on to that already holding the candle in place.

As with many new crafts, it is advisable for the organiser to try it out before attempting to work with a group of students. In that way, many pitfalls which might be encountered can be planned for and the session will progress more smoothly.

Candlemaking can become quite an obsession and there are many pieces of equipment to invest in and ideas to try for those who wish to take up the craft as a hobby.

15 Patchwork Tea-cosy

A tea-cosy may be classed as an old-fashioned item but it makes a useful as well as a colourful gift. This simple hexagon pattern will give an introduction to the traditional needlecraft of patchwork.

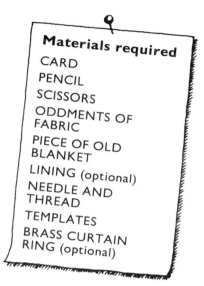

Materials required
CARD
PENCIL
SCISSORS
ODDMENTS OF FABRIC
PIECE OF OLD BLANKET
LINING (optional)
NEEDLE AND THREAD
TEMPLATES
BRASS CURTAIN RING (optional)

METHOD

1. Trace the shapes at the end of this chapter, transfer them to card and cut them out to use as templates.

2. Use your templates to draw out the correct number of pieces on to card and cut them out. You will need 7 complete hexagons, 6 half-hexagons and 4 three-quarter-hexagons for each side.

Take great care to be as accurate as possible with each pencil line and scissor cut, as any error or inaccuracy at this stage will be magnified when the pieces are put together and the cosy will not fit properly.

3. Iron the oddments of fabric you have chosen to use and cut fabric, for each patch, 2 cm larger all round than the cardboard shape.

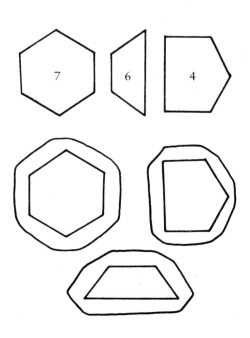

4. Work on one shape at a time, folding the material over the edges and using tacking stitches to keep it in place. Keep the stitching as tight as possible, especially at each corner.

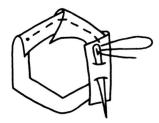

5. When you have covered all the pieces for the first side of the tea-cosy, arrange them in your chosen design and begin stitching them together. If using a flower pattern, begin at the centre of the flower and work outwards; if creating a striped design, begin at one side of the cosy and work, in stripes, from one side to the other.

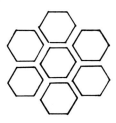

6. Take the first two pieces, place them right sides together, and sew along the edge to be joined. Use small oversew stitches from one point to the other, finishing off securely. Try not to catch the card in your stitches as this will make it difficult to remove the card pieces when the cosy is complete.

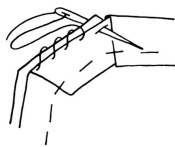

7. When the edge is finished, open the patchwork pieces and flatten them.

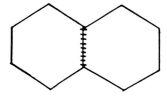

8. Place the next piece in position (face down on top of the last one) and sew them together, as before.

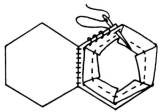

9. Sew as many pieces as possible in this manner. You will come to some patches which cannot be placed face downwards on another. Sew these by holding them flat, side by side, and oversewing at the back, as close to the edges as possible.

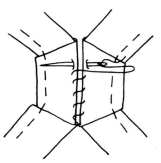

10. When the pattern is complete and all the pieces have been sewn together, place the work on an ironing board, right side uppermost, cover it with a dry cloth and press with a hot iron.

11. Use the same method to make the second side of the cosy.

12. Fit the two sides of the cosy together – right sides inside – and, using oversew stitches, join them together – up one side, over the top and down the other side, leaving the bottom open.

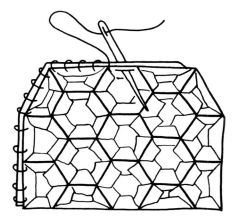

13. Lay the finished patchwork on the blanket. Cut two pieces of blanket to the shape of the tea-cosy, leaving enough around the edges to turn in neatly. If the blanket is thin, you may wish to cut it double, so that there are two thicknesses on each side of the cosy.

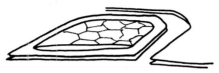

14. Join the blanket shapes along both sides and across the top. Use a back-stitch, if hand sewing, or do this on the sewing machine. Stitch fairly near the edge so that the inside of the cosy does not become too bulky.

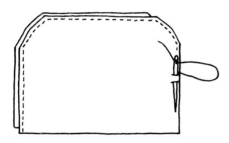

15. Slide the blanket over the tea-cosy. Turn and pin up the bottom edge of the blanket so that it fits the patchwork.

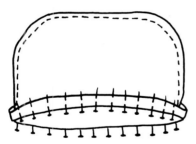

16. Remove the blanket for the time being and carefully take out all the cards from the patchwork. Iron it.

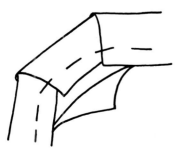

17. Fit the blanket over the patchwork and sew the bottom edge, all round, using small oversew or slip-hemming stitches.

18. Complete the work by turning the cosy right side out and sew a line of very small running stitches up one side, over the top and down the other side to anchor the blanket to the patchwork. Try to keep these stitches small, especially on the outside, so that they do not detract from the patchwork pattern.

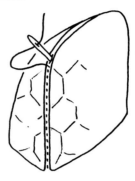

19. If lining the tea-cosy, repeat the method of making up and inserting the blanket, but this time use a piece of lining material.

20. To finish, a brass curtain ring can be covered and sewn to the top of the cosy so that it can be hung up when not in use. Cover the ring with a matching embroidery thread or wool, using blanket stitch.

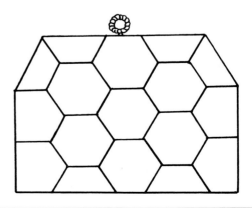

ORGANISING YOUR MATERIALS

I. Setting up the work area

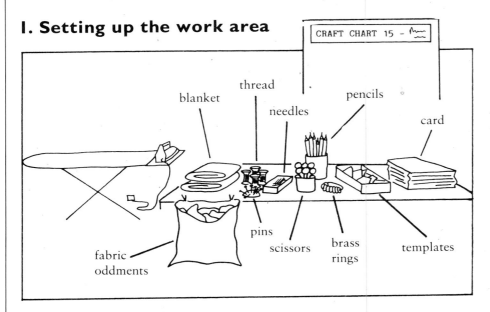

CRAFT CHART 15 –

blanket thread needles pencils card pins scissors brass rings templates fabric oddments

Provide the basic materials like card, pencils, scissors, needle and thread, but ask students to make their own choices of fabric by bringing items from home. If space is limited, suggest that all material is ironed before being brought along for the session. If equipment such as pencils and scissors is in short supply, organise the groupwork so that each student draws, cuts and sews, producing finished patches as the session progresses, thus releasing equipment for others to use. If all students are expected to draw out the patches and cut them at the same time, it will be necessary to provide a pencil and scissors per student or some will lose interest through being kept waiting.

2. Templates

Use card which will hold its shape when the material has been sewn round it, not card which will bend too easily. Cereal packets are quite good for this purpose; 'best' card is unnecessary. If treated with respect, the cards can be reused for other patchwork later on.

It is most important that the drawing and cutting of the hexagons is done accurately as this will affect the finished work. Students will require 14 hexagons, 12 half-hexagons and 8 $\frac{3}{4}$-hexagons per tea-cosy. They should be encouraged to write their names (or initials) on each patch cut out so that the name is visible when the material has been sewn on. One or two patches are sure to be mislaid and there will be no arguments as to whose they are if names are clearly written on them.

3. Fabric

Any fabric may be used for patchwork but keep in mind the necessity for washing the tea-cosy in the months to come. Cottons, rayons, linens and most synthetic fibres are best. Do not include heavy materials like wool or very light fabrics like organza, if the rest of the cosy is cotton. Any piece of fabric which is likely to shrink when washed will only spoil the shape of the cosy and should not be used.

A good way of gathering fabric is to ask each student to bring an old summer frock (preferably taken to pieces and ironed before being brought along) and these can be 'pooled' to provide a wide choice of colours and designs. Some schools may keep a 'bit-bag' which can be used for patchwork.

4. Needles and thread

An ordinary sewing needle (Sharps No. 7) is adequate for patchwork. Some needles are rather thick and, although they have a large eye for threading, they will leave an unnecessarily large hole in the material.

A good hint for threading a needle is to moisten the end of the thread and hold it steady in the fingers of one hand whilst bringing the eye of the needle down on to it with the other hand.

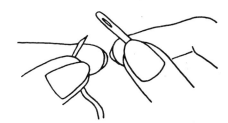

Use ordinary sewing thread in a variety of colours so that students can choose the one which suits their colour schemes. It is not necessary to be too pedantic in using tacking cotton for covering the patches and 'best' cotton for making up the patchwork; this will depend on the availability of these types of thread.

5. Blanket

The purpose of this is, obviously, to insulate the cosy to keep the teapot warm, so the thicker the blanket, the fewer layers will be needed. Students may be able to supply their own pieces of blanket; alternatively, keep your eyes open at school fairs or the local Oxfam shop for fairly cheap blankets which can be washed and used for a number of students.

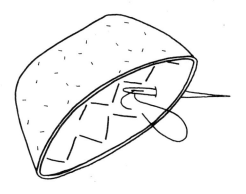

The blanket can be anchored to the patchwork, not only along the top and sides, but by using stay-stitching across the middle of the cosy. This should show on the inside as long tacking stitches, but not show at all on the patchwork itself.

6. Lining

Choose a lining material which will suit the other materials used in the patchwork, both in colour and composition. Old curtaining is often useful for this purpose and quite a number of tea-cosies can be lined from one curtain. Lining is not vital, but does give a finished piece of work. Anchoring the lining at the top and sides (inside) should be sufficient to hold it in place. Make sure that it is not too tight for the size of the cosy.

7. Ring

To enable the cosy to be hung up when not in use, cover a brass curtain ring (preferably one which is continuous and has no split) with blanket stitching. Use embroidery thread, or even wool, in a colour which will fit with the overall scheme of the cosy. Sew this to the top of the tea-cosy to complete the work.

8. Accuracy

As previously stated, the drawing and cutting of the cardboard shapes must be done accurately as this will affect the way the patchwork fits together. Each small deviation, though considered minor on its own, will only be magnified when the whole is assembled.

If students are to trace the templates with ruler and pencil, or if they are to draw their own hexagons, based on a circle, there is one golden rule which they must remember:

It is the pencil that draws the line, not the ruler.

Aligning the ruler to the two points means that the pencil will mark a line *above* the points.

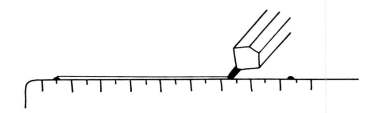

To draw a straight line which starts in the middle of one point and finishes in the middle of the second point, first place the *pencil* on point 1, sliding the ruler up to fit snugly against it. Place the pencil exactly on point 2 and slide the other end of the ruler to fit under the pencil. As the ruler may have moved slightly during this last adjustment, *test* the two points again, or even a third time, until it is certain that the pencil will leave one point and make straight for the second.

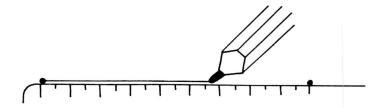

This may seem quite a palaver merely to draw a straight line but, in any area where accuracy will affect the finished work, it is well worth taking the extra trouble to ensure that each element of the work is completed as accurately as possible.

SUGGESTIONS FOR DESIGNS

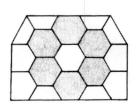 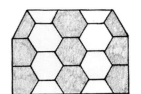 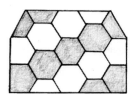

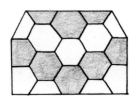 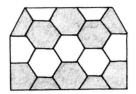

TEMPLATES FOR PATCHWORK

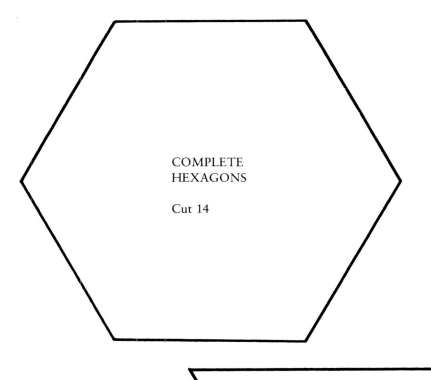

COMPLETE
HEXAGONS

Cut 14

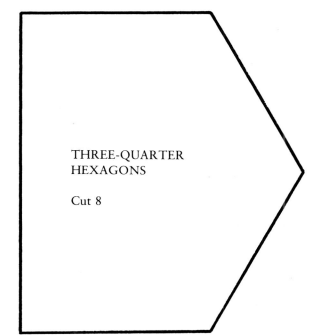

THREE-QUARTER
HEXAGONS

Cut 8

HALF HEXAGONS

Cut 12

16 Pop-up Puppets

Pop-up puppets are an unusual variation on a well-loved toy. Follow the instructions for a seasonal Santa Claus who disappears into the chimney, or use the basic idea to create your own hide-away puppet.

METHOD

1. Wash and dry the pot so that it is clean. Make a hole in the base, large enough for the dowel to thread through easily.

 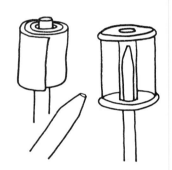

2. If the dowel is too thick to fit into the centre of the cotton reel, shave one end with a craft knife and glue it in place.

If the dowel is not thick enough and keeps slipping out, glue a strip of paper around the end of the dowel until it is fat enough to glue and hold in position.

3. Trace the pattern for Santa's jacket and cut out two from white paper. The bottom edge of his jacket will fit around the top of the yoghurt pot, so make sure that each pattern will stretch half-way round the pot, with a little to spare. Make the pattern wider at the bottom, if necessary.

4. The neck edge of his jacket should fit around the cotton reel, so make sure that each pattern piece will stretch half-way round the cotton reel, with a little to spare. Make the pattern wider at the top, if necessary.

When you are sure the pattern will fit, cut two from red fabric.

5. Trace the patterns for Santa's hands, which can be found at the end of this chapter, and cut out two from pink fabric.

6. Glue one hand to the end of each sleeve on one half of the jacket.

7. Run a line of glue from the neck edge, along the sleeve, over the hand and down the body of the jacket and glue the pair together *on one side only*.

8. Run a line of glue along the bottom edge of Santa's jacket and fix this in place around the top of the pot. Pinch the jacket together at the join and pat the fabric firmly to fit it to the pot.

9. Thread the dowel through the hole in the pot and glue the neck edge of the jacket around the bottom of the cotton reel. Pinch the fabric together at the join and pat the jacket to the cotton reel so that it holds firmly.

10. Apply a line of glue to the open edge of the jacket and sleeve and fix the two halves together to join him up completely.

Allow all the glue to 'take' before trying him out!

11. While the glue is drying, trace the pattern for the pot cover, which can be found at the end of this chapter. Cut the pattern out from white paper and test it round the yoghurt pot to make sure it fits.

Mark the paper with a pencil where any adjustment needs to be made. Keep cutting or making other paper patterns until you are sure that the pattern will fit the pot exactly, with just a small overlap at the side and bottom.

12. Use the pattern to cut out the pot cover from red fabric. Glue this to the yoghurt pot – the join coming at the back – and glue the bottom edge under the pot to make a neat finish.

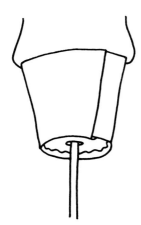

13. With glue, draw three rings around the pot and pat black wool on to the glue.

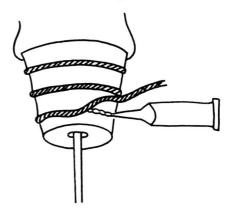

14. Draw lines of glue, downwards, between the rings and fit short lengths of black wool in place, to form the brickwork of the chimney.

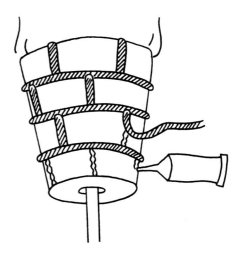

15. Trace the pattern for Santa's head and transfer it to white paper. Make sure that it is big enough to go right round the cotton reel with a small overlap.

Cut the pattern from pink fabric and glue this around the cotton reel (with the join coming at the back). Press the top edge over and glue the circle in place to neaten it.

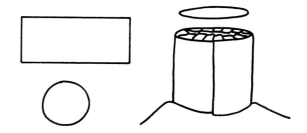

16. Trace the pattern for Santa's hat. Cut out the hat from red fabric and cut along the dotted line.

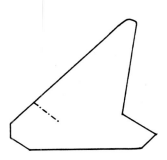

17. Apply a line of glue to the long edge and the two short sides adjacent.

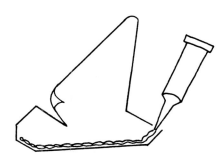

18. Attach the hat to the covered cotton reel, just like a headscarf, as illustrated.

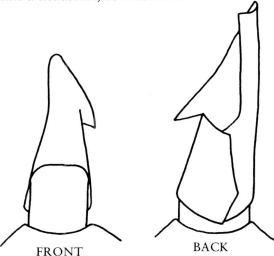

FRONT   BACK

19. Bend the point to one side and apply glue to the long edges of the point. Press them together, starting at the point and working towards the head.

BACK

20. Pad the top of his hat with a little cotton wool, tissue or small pieces of fabric.

21. Glue down the remaining tab to neaten the back.

The point can be glued to Santa's head and the white pom-pom fixed to the end of the point once his hair has been glued in place.

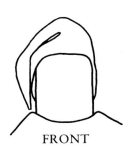 

FRONT   BACK

22. Trace the pattern for Santa's hair and whiskers. Cut the shape from white paper first and make any adjustment necessary.

Cut the shape from white fabric and glue it in place to make his face.

23. Finish the puppet by adding further decoration – a white fabric circle for the end of his hat; a black belt with a shiny buckle; eyes made from pieces of fabric or sequins; extra hair, cut from the white fabric.

Leave the finished puppet to dry completely before you begin to play with it.

ORGANISING YOUR MATERIALS

1. Setting up the work area

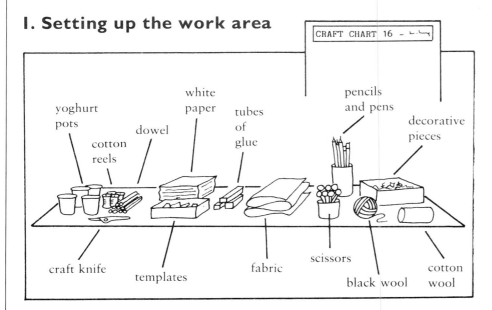

This particular piece of craftwork offers a wide variety of choice in the materials which can be used. Those mentioned here are simply suggestions and any number of alternatives can be used, depending on availability.

2. Yoghurt pots

These are fairly easy to obtain and children should be able to supply their own for the session or have collected sufficient, in advance.

If intending to use this idea with younger children, it is recommended that enough pots are collected beforehand so that they can be prepared – cleaned and the hole put in the centre – before being given out to the group.

Some yoghurt pots are made from a plastic which is easily pierced with a drawing pin, so that one point of a pair of scissors can be inserted and worked round to make a hole large enough for the dowel to pass through. This does take a few minutes and it is best to prepare the pots in advance so that children do not need to wield scissors and pins in this way.

Some pots are made from a very much thicker plastic which tends to crack rather than pare away. These pots can still be used but a better method of making the hole is with a hot instrument. If there is a soldering iron handy, heat this in the usual way and just push it gently through the bottom of the pot, allowing the heat to melt the plastic as it goes. It is *not* recommended that children be allowed to do this for themselves, and whoever prepares the pots in this way should ensure that it is done in a well-ventilated room as fumes from melting plastic can be dangerous.

There are many sizes of yoghurt pot. The patterns for the chimney covering and Santa's jacket, which can be found at the end of this chapter, are based on a 150 g Ski yoghurt pot which is only slightly tapered. It is advisable to try to collect pots of a similar brand and for the organiser to adjust the pattern to fit that type of pot, before preparing any patterns or templates for the group to use.

Most yoghurt pots have a lip all round. Do not be tempted to cut this ring away as this will ruin the stability and firmness of the rim.

3. Dowel

Rods of dowel can be purchased, quite inexpensively, from most do-it-yourself shops and then cut to the required length, using a sharp craft knife. Mark the dowel with a pencil where it needs to be cut, lay it on a piece of board to protect the work surface and roll it under the knife, so that it is cut all the way round.

If the diameter of the dowel is bigger than the hole through the centre of the cotton reel, pare the end of the dowel with a sharp knife so that it can be glued into place. Again, these dowels should be prepared in advance to prevent the need for children to sharpen the ends of the sticks.

If the dowel has a slightly smaller diameter than the cotton reel, which means that the stick keeps falling out, glue a strip of paper around the end of the dowel until it is padded enough to fill out the hole in the cotton reel. Glue this into position. Try to leave enough time for the glue to dry at this stage, or the join between the dowel and the cotton reel will remain a weak point of the puppet.

4. Templates

Making templates for a group of children to draw round is by far the easiest way of providing patterns for craftwork. Simply trace the patterns, transfer them to white paper and test them against the size of pot which will be used. Make any adjustments necessary and, when satisfied that the patterns will work, cut them from card. It is not necessary to provide a set for each child, but do ensure that there are sufficient templates to keep them all busy without having to wait for long.

Adjustments may need to be made in the following areas:
- the neck of Santa's jacket (to fit the cotton reel);
- the hem of Santa's jacket (to fit the pot);
- the circle and rectangle (which cover the cotton reel);
- the pot cover (which makes the chimney).

5. Glue

Use a strong, impact glue for this work. PVA glue is not suitable, as it is water-based and would be absorbed by the fabric. Use a UHU glue or similar brand but remember that this type of adhesive leaves 'strings' when applied so can be far more messy than gums, paste and PVA. Remember, too, that spirit-based adhesives have a smell and should be used in a well-ventilated room.

It will be necessary to provide one tube of UHU for each small group – probably one tube for three students – as the tubes won't last long.

6. Fabric

As the fabric will be glued into place, the risk of fraying will be minimal, so most types of fabric will be suitable for the Santa Claus. Felt, which is a bonded material, is the best type of fabric to use but this can be expensive.

Using a white fur fabric for the hair, whiskers and trim around the base of the Santa will give a really good finish to the work but some fur fabrics will shed their fur when cut and it is advisable to test a small piece before letting the students use it. Fur fabric which sheds its nap will look fine at the start but soon become bald and the children will be disappointed with the result. However, the glue should hold most of the fur in place and children should be encouraged to handle the cut pieces as little as possible.

Instead of white fur fabric, choose a fairly substantial brand of cotton wool and glue pieces to the Santa's face, jacket and hat. However, do note that cotton wool is quite delicate and will probably be more easily damaged when Santa is 'potted' and 'de-potted'.

7. Black wool

Any ply of black wool is suitable. This can also be used for Santa's buttons: knot the wool two or three times in the same place, make a large knot, cut this off from the remaining wool and glue the knot on to the front of his jacket.

It can also be used to make his belt by finger-knitting the wool to form a length which will fit around his middle. (See Chapter 19 for the instructions on finger-knitting).

TEMPLATES FOR SANTA CLAUS

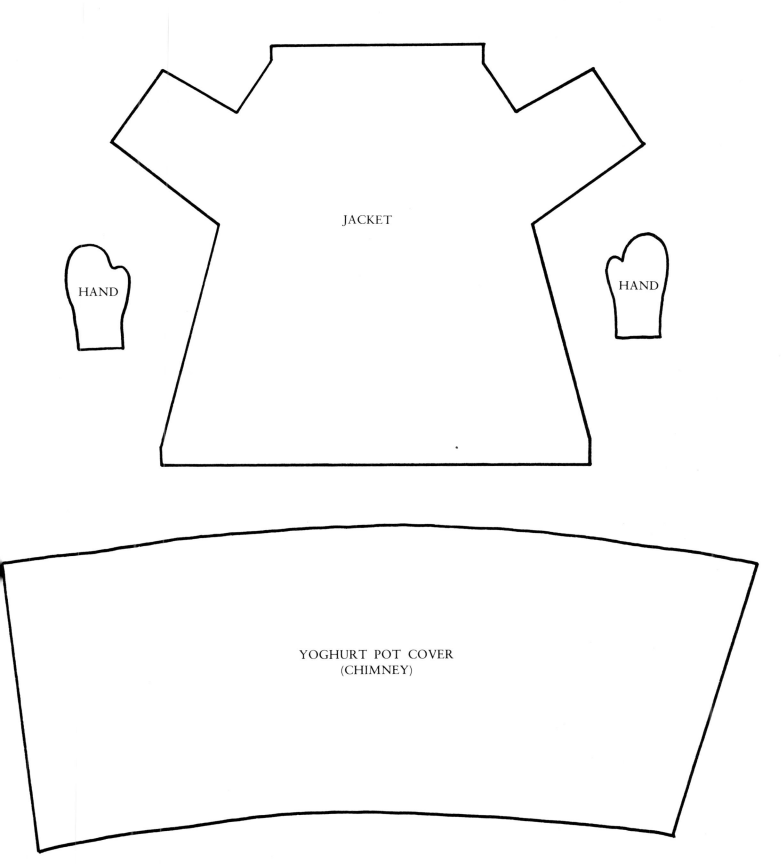

JACKET

HAND

HAND

YOGHURT POT COVER
(CHIMNEY)

TEMPLATES FOR SANTA CLAUS

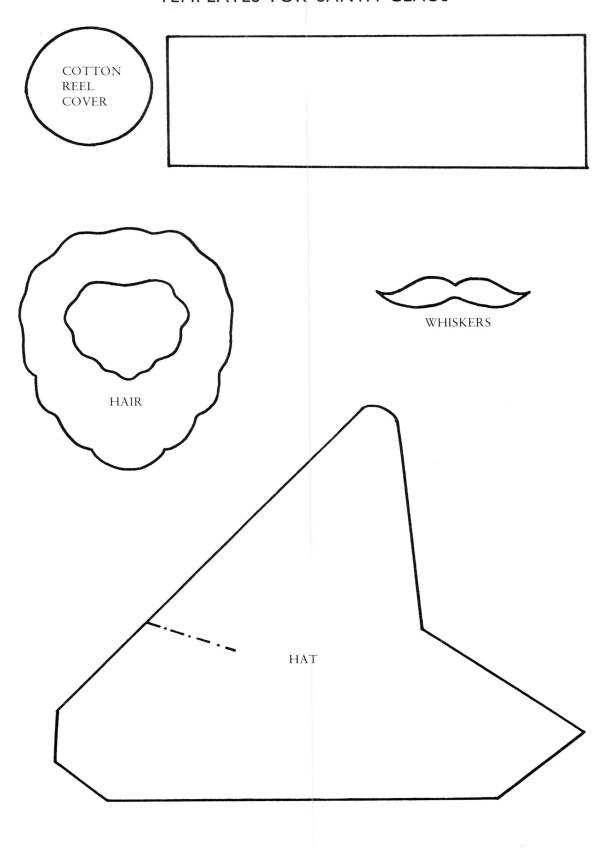

COTTON
REEL
COVER

HAIR

WHISKERS

HAT

17 Découpage Piggy Bank

Découpage work was very popular with the Victorians, who used it to decorate small boxes for jewellery and other treasures. Their work was far more intricate than this piggy bank but based on the same technique of decorating with cut-out shapes and varnishing over.

Materials required

Stage 1
PLASTIC BOTTLE (with handle)
EGG-BOX
NEWSPAPER
COLD-WATER PASTE
BRUSH
CRAFT KNIFE
SCISSORS
SELLOTAPE

Stage 2
PAINT
BRUSHES
WHITE CARD
PVA ADHESIVE
HOLE PUNCH (optional)
VARNISH
COLOURED PIPE CLEANER
TWEEZERS
WHITE SPIRIT
PENCIL
PATTERNS

METHOD

1. Make sure that the bottle has been washed and is perfectly dry. With the craft knife, cut off the handle at its base and top. This will leave a flattened shape for the pig's face.

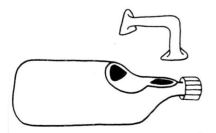

2. Cut a slit in the back for the money to go in. This will be neatened by one of the decorative card pieces (see patterns at the end of this chapter) but make sure that the slit is large enough to allow all sizes of money to pass through.

3. Cut two pieces of card, slightly larger than the holes left by the handle, and sellotape these cards over the holes to make a flat surface.

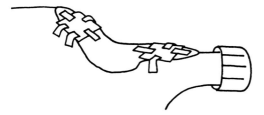

4. Cut two egg wells from the egg-box and sellotape these into place to make the pig's eyes.

5. Cut four more egg wells from the egg-box and sellotape these in place to form the feet. You will find that the pig will be rather front-heavy so experiment with the positioning of the feet until it balances and is in proportion.

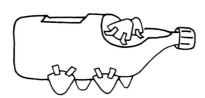

6. Trace the pattern for the ears at the end of this chapter and cut two ears from card. Cut along the centre of each ear, as marked on the pattern, and overlap the edges so that the ear bends forward slightly. Glue the overlap to hold the position and, when dry, sellotape the ears in place on the pig's forehead.

7. Tear the white edges from some of the sheets of newspaper and then tear the strips into small squares of approximately 1–2 cm. Keep these to one side, separately.

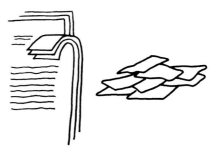

8. Tear the newspaper into strips and then into squares of a similar size to the white ones and keep these separately.

9. Mix up the cold-water paste – as you would for wallpaper – and begin the papier mâché work from the pile of newspaper squares, using the brush to lift one square at a time and pasting it on to the bottle.

10. Use your fingers to neaten the edges of the ears (smaller pieces of paper will make a neater job here) and press well down with the brush, as you work, to make as smooth a surface as possible, all over.

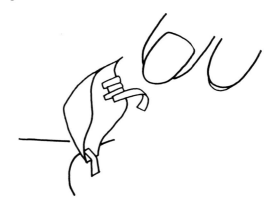

11. The squares should overlap so that no part of the bottle (except the screw thread) shows when the newspaper layer has been completed.

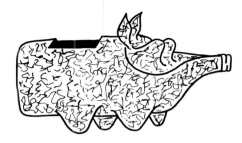

12. Now repeat the papier mâché work, this time using the white squares. Go over *every* part again, so that no newspaper is left showing when the layer is finished.

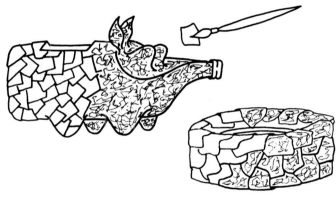

13. Paste two layers of papier mâché (first in newspaper and then in white paper) to the bottle top. Fold the edges of the paper neatly over the rim so that they hold the covering in place but do not hinder the working of the threads.

14. When all the papier mâché is dry, paint the piggy's eyes with white paint and the remainder (plus the bottle top) in a bright colour.

15. Include the tops of the pig's eyes when using the coloured paint, so that you give it eyelids.

16. Cut two strips of card (approximately 4 cm wide) which are long enough to stretch along the eyelids to form lashes.

Fold the card along its length, 1 cm from the edge – this is the strip which will be attached to the eyelids.

Fringe the lashes and curl them with closed scissors. Paint them black and, when dry, attach one to each eyelid.

17. Trace the découpage patterns at the end of this chapter and transfer them to white card.

Each shape has two parts, a white background and a slightly smaller coloured insert.

Cut out all the shapes and put to one side all those which are to remain white. Paint the smaller, middle shapes and leave these to dry.

18. Using the PVA adhesive, stick the white background shapes into position. Begin with the money slit, the large flower, its leaves and stalk. Use the smaller flowers to fill in gaps, as required.

Refer to the illustrations when positioning the white pieces and fixing the coloured shapes.

19. Use a hole punch to make the decorative dots which go on to the large flower petals and the money slit. A pair of tweezers will help with the handling of these very small dots.

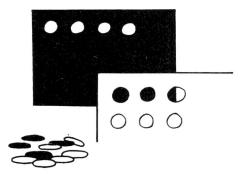

20. Punch two holes in the centre decoration of the snout. The area which shows through these holes can be painted black for the nostrils.

21. Build up the tail as shown in the diagram. Wind the coloured pipe cleaner around your finger to form the curl.

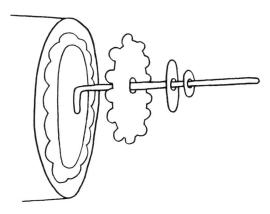

22. When all the glue is dry, apply a coat of polyurethane varnish to finish the work.

ORGANISING YOUR MATERIALS

I. Setting up the work area

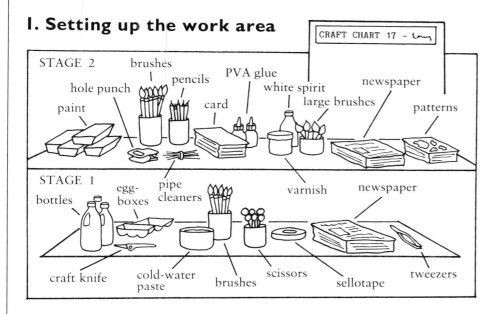

Set up the work area, in the first instance, for papier mâché work. This will take a number of sessions to complete so the painting and varnishing area will not be required at the initial stage. Some students will complete the papier mâché well before others so, if space is limited, encourage them to prepare their découpage shapes before beginning to paint. This will give the remaining students an opportunity to finish the papier mâché and the equipment can be cleared before setting out the painting and varnishing materials. This may work, in principle, but be prepared for an overlap if some students are much slower than others.

2. Newspaper

A more detailed description of papier mâché work can be found in Chapter 10. However, the organiser is reminded here that the reason for separating the white edges of the newspaper from the printed part is so that students can use two 'colours' of newspaper and be able to tell, just by looking at the work, where they have got to. This prevents some areas of the work getting two coats at the expense of other parts.

By using a layer of printed newspaper first, the second, white layer will provide a clear background on which to paint, allowing the full brightness of the colour to show.

Newspaper is by far the best type of paper to use for this work as, being so absorbent, it will bond together with the paste to make a really solid coating. An alternative type of white paper may be used but do ensure that this is also absorbent or extra difficulties may be encountered in moulding the paper to the shapes required – especially those round the edges of the ears and at the rim of the bottle top.

Ideally, more than two layers of papier mâché should be used. Four coats (newspaper/white/newspaper/white) would give a more firm base, but as the work is so large children may lose interest, and by the time they have completed two layers of papier mâché, they will be keen to start on the next stage.

3. Cold-water paste

Use either a normal strength wallpaper paste or a similar medium available through educational suppliers. Please note that other liquid gums and glues are far too sticky for papier mâché and should *not* be used for this part of the craftwork.

Cold-water paste can be made up in a large container and decanted into smaller pots for each group. Sealing the containers at the close of each session will ensure that the paste is workable for the next time.

No special brushes are necessary for cold-water paste. Use a fairly large, clean paintbrush but ensure that it is washed well at the end of each session. As the paste is water-based the brush should clean quickly and completely in warm water.

4. Bottle

Use any size of polythene bottle which has been washed and dried. It may be advisable for the organiser to prepare these in advance by cutting off the handles and making the slit for the money as this will dispense with the need for children to use craft knives. Keep one bottle intact to show the group how the handle was cut and the slit made. This can be demonstrated at the beginning of the first session and then the prepared bottles handed out. When removing the handles, cut as low as possible in order to leave a really flat surface for the face.

5. Egg-boxes

Any type of egg-box may be used. The polystyrene ones have a much rounder well and look more authentic than those made from recycled card, which tend to have ridges or faces. However, the papier mâché does stick better to the recyled card as this is absorbent. Children must be less 'heavy-handed' when covering the polystyrene type to prevent the pieces of newspaper from slipping. Once the papier mâché is dry, it will bond just as well over either sort.

6. Card

Choose a card which is easy for the children to handle and cut but which will keep its shape when

varnished. It may be necessary to roll the card gently in the hands to encourage it into the curve of the bottle. Do not bend or crease it as this will detract from the finished effect.

To conserve the card, cut templates of the shapes for the children to draw round and encourage them to place each shape as close as possible to the previous one. Alternatively, the organiser may decide to draw the shapes in advance and present each child with a set ready to cut out. Although this is time-consuming, it may be advisable if card is scarce.

7. Paint

Use a powder or ready-mix paint to which a generous squeeze of PVA adhesive has been added. The glue not only helps to thicken the paint but also gives it an added resistance to 'running' when the varnish is applied. If mixed to a fairly thick consistency, one coat only should be needed to cover the papier mâché. Give each child a sheet of newspaper on which to stand the piggy for painting. If the paint is thick it should be possible to paint the back and face first and for these to be dry enough to turn the work upside down by the time they get to the feet. The bottle top (the snout) should be painted in the same colour as the main body part.

Use a similar mix of paints for the coloured inserts in the découpage. Ensure that the paint is applied to the sides of the shapes as well as the top and place them on a clean sheet of newspaper to dry. Children can put their initials on the back of each piece, before painting, so that no arguments arise if one is mislaid!

Mix the paint and glue in clean margarine tubs, with lids (one tub for each colour) as these can be sealed after use and the paint will stay in a workable condition for some weeks. The tubs can be 'topped up' when necessary and, if the paint and glue separate through standing, a good stir with a brush or spoon will bring them back to a working consistency very quickly. Mark a line of the paint on the lid to denote which colour the tub contains.

8. Glue

Use the same type of PVA adhesive for attaching the découpage decorations to the painted body of the pig. As PVA glue dries to a transparent finish, any excess glue will disappear when dry. It also gives the opportunity of 'sliding' the pattern into position if it has been placed too high or low and gives time to adjust the coloured inserts to the required place.

9. Pipe cleaners

Coloured pipe cleaners can be obtained from craft shops or most educational suppliers. If unavailable, use a piece of cord or card, or let the students invent their own means of making a tail for their pigs. Thread the chosen tail through the tail decorations as shown in the diagram earlier and attach it to the pig's bottom before gluing the decorative pieces in place.

10. Patterns

Trace the patterns for the découpage which can be found at the end of this chapter and transfer them to card to make templates for the children to draw round.

Alternatively, older students can be given the patterns as they are on the sheets, and can make their own templates. Remember that some shapes are to remain white and these should be put to one side while the other, smaller ones are painted.

Use the small flowers as extra decoration, making as many as necessary to fill in any gaps. The larger the bottle, the more gaps there may be. Create an

opportunity for individuality by inviting students to make up their own flowers, using the ideas given.

11. Varnish

Use a polyurethane varnish which can be obtained from most paint stores. This comes in fairly large amounts and can be decanted into smaller jars for resealing after use. Apply the varnish with a large brush, using long, even strokes and a light touch so that the brush has as little contact with the paintwork as possible.

Begin with the white eyes, the face and along the pig's back, gradually working downwards. Use enough varnish to give a shiny coat but not so much that the varnish runs and leaves the pig looking streaky!

It is quite a good idea to apply the varnish in two stages, leaving the feet until the back is dry. The model can then be turned upside down and the underside varnished to join up. In this way there will be fewer problems in handling the model while it is wet and finding somewhere to leave it to dry.

Polyurethane varnish is spirit-based and the brushes used for varnishing will require turps or white spirit for cleaning. If not cleaned properly after each session, these brushes will be useless.

MONEY SLIT

white background

coloured insert

Affix pieces as shown, gluing small dots to coloured insert.

SIDE SWIRLS

coloured inserts

white backgrounds

Affix pieces as shown, either side of the large flower.

DÉCOUPAGE PATTERNS FOR TRACING

LARGE FLOWER

white background

coloured insert

white background

coloured insert

Affix pieces as shown, arranging white dots around the edges of the coloured petals.

SMALL FLOWER (1)

white background

coloured insert

white background

coloured insert

white background

coloured insert

Affix pieces as shown.

DÉCOUPAGE PATTERNS FOR TRACING

SMALL FLOWER (2)

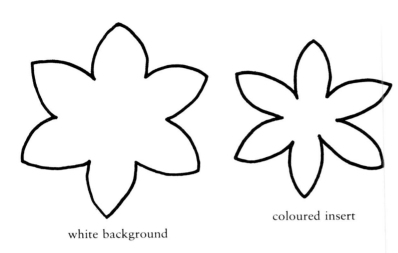

white background

coloured insert

white
background

coloured
insert

*Affix pieces as shown and make
as many as required to fill in
any gaps which need decoration.*

THE SNOUT

white background

coloured insert

*Affix pieces as shown, painting
the shaded area black and punching
two holes in the coloured
insert to make the nostrils.*

PIGGY'S EARS

*Cut out patterns in
card and make up
as described.*

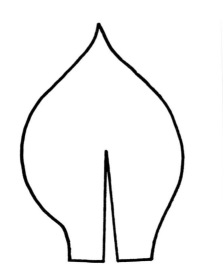

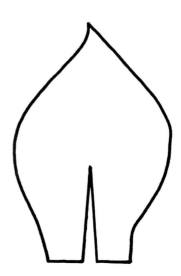

DÉCOUPAGE PATTERNS FOR TRACING

THE TAIL

coloured inner ring

coloured outer ring

coloured rings

Affix pieces as shown, threading the coloured pipe cleaner through the holes and gluing it to the base of the bottle.

18 Knitted Moccasins

Knitted moccasins are very simple to make and teach the basic knitting stitches. More elaborate moccasins can be produced by using a patterned stitch, adding a crocheted top border or embroidering a design on the completed slippers.

Materials required

DOUBLE-KNITTING WOOL

PAIR OF KNITTING NEEDLES

CONTRASTING WOOL FOR POM-POM

DARNING NEEDLE

INSOLE OR LEATHERETTE

PAPER, PENCIL AND FELT PEN

SCISSORS

METHOD

1. Buy a pair of insoles which fit your feet or make a pair of soles from leatherette, in the following way.

2. Stand on a piece of white paper and draw round your left foot.

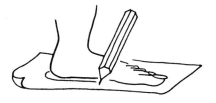

3. Go over the line smoothing out all the 'bumps' and cut out the shape.

4. Using the shape as a template, transfer it to a piece of leatherette and cut it out.

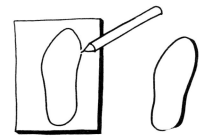

5. Turn the pattern over and draw and cut out the shape for the other foot.

Put these to one side to use later.

6. With double-knitting wool and a pair of needles, cast on one stitch. Work in garter stitch throughout.

7.

Row 1:	Cast on 1 stitch.	(1 st)
Row 2:	Increase in stitch.	(2 sts)
Row 3:	Knit 1, increase in last stitch.	(3 sts)
Row 4:	Increase in first stitch, Knit 2.	(4 sts)
Row 5:	Knit 3, increase in last stitch.	(5 sts)
Row 6:	Increase in first stitch, Knit 4.	(6 sts)
Row 7:	Knit 5, increase in last stitch.	(7 sts)
Row 8:	Increase in first stitch, Knit 6.	(8 sts)
Row 9:	Knit 7, increase in last stitch.	(9 sts)
Row 10:	Increase in first stitch, Knit 8.	(10 sts)
Row 11:	Knit 9, increase in last stitch.	(11 sts)
Row 12:	Increase in first stitch, Knit 10.	(12 sts)
Row 13:	Knit 11, increase in last stitch.	(13 sts)
Row 14:	Increase in first stitch, Knit 12.	(14 sts)
Row 15:	Knit 13, increase in last stitch.	(15 sts)
Row 16:	Increase in first stitch, Knit 14.	(16 sts)
Row 17:	Knit 15, increase in last stitch.	(17 sts)
Row 18:	Increase in first stitch, Knit 16.	(18 sts)
Row 19:	Knit 17, increase in last stitch.	(19 sts)
Row 20:	Increase in first stitch, Knit 18.	(20 sts)

The work should look like a right-angled triangle, rising at an angle on one side only.

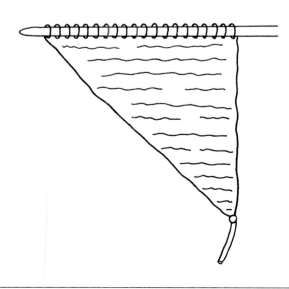

8. Continue knitting, in garter stitch, on these 20 stitches until the strip is long enough to go round the first insole, measuring from the point.

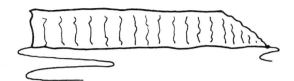

9. Cast off, leaving a long end.

10. Knit another strip to match, for the other moccasin.

11. Join each strip into a ring by oversewing the straight cast-off edge to the line of increasing.

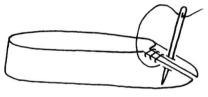

12. If making your own insoles, pierce holes through the leatherette about 4 mm from the edge, all the way round.

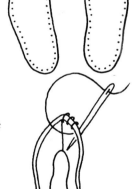

13. Beginning at the point of the knitting, sew the moccasin to the insole, stretching it evenly all round. Make up the second moccasin in the same way.

14. Plait or finger-knit a cord and weave this through the top of the knitting. Make a full pom-pom (see Chapter 6 for the method) and attach one to each end of the tie.

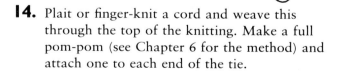

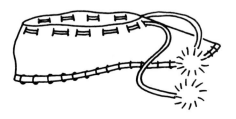

ORGANISING YOUR MATERIALS

I. Setting up the work area

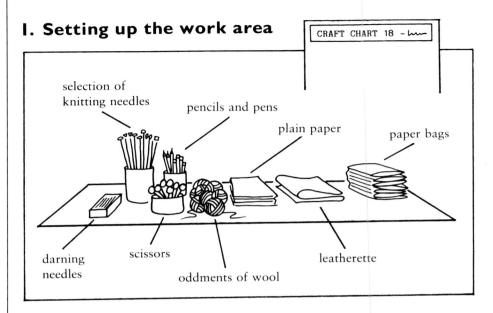

CRAFT CHART 18 - ﹌

selection of knitting needles

pencils and pens

plain paper

paper bags

darning needles

scissors

oddments of wool

leatherette

2. Knitting needles

Any fairly large size of knitting needle can be used for this task. It is not necessary that every child in the group works with the same size (providing, of course, that each has a matching pair!!) The sizing of needles has changed over the past few years. They used to be gauged by numbers (the lower the number the fatter the needle) but are now measured according to the diameter in millimetres. The following table may be of use when sorting out an old stock of knitting needles.

UK	000	00	0	I	2	3	4	5	6	7	8	9	10	II	12	13	14
American	15	13	12	11	$10\frac{1}{2}$	10	9	8	7	6	5	4	3	2	1	0	00
mm metric	10	9	8	$7\frac{1}{2}$	7	$6\frac{1}{2}$	6	$5\frac{1}{2}$	5	$4\frac{1}{2}$	4	$3\frac{3}{4}$	$3\frac{1}{4}$	3	$2\frac{3}{4}$	$2\frac{1}{4}$	2

It is recommended that needles are chosen within the 6 mm–$4\frac{1}{2}$ mm range (old sizes 4–7); for example, a pair of $5\frac{1}{2}$ mm (5) needles will give a strip of knitting 10 cm wide on 20 stitches in double-knitting wool. Obviously the knitting will vary according to the size of needle and the thickness of wool. Be prepared to adjust the number of stitches or rows. Luckily, these moccasins offer as wide a range of possibilities as there are sizes of children's feet!

3. Wool

Although double-knitting wool is recommended (it is easy for children to handle and it 'grows' quickly), there is no reason why a different ply of wool should not be used.

If you consider that the wool you have available is too fine, suggest that a child uses two strands at once – either of the same colour or two contrasting colours.

These moccasins are a useful way to use up oddments of wool and can even be made in stripes of different colours if large balls of wool are not available. Many mothers (and most grandmothers) knit and children might be able to provide their own wool fairly easily.

4. Darning needles

Darning needles are suggested for sewing the mocassins and attaching the soles, but any needle with a large eye can be used. Ensure that the needle is not so big that it damages the leatherette by tearing the holes as they are sewn.

5. Leatherette

Off-cuts of leatherette can be obtained at many fabric stores and upholsterers and the shopkeeper will often agree to a 'special offer' once he knows what it is for.

Leatherette usually has a coloured, shiny side and a backing of either rubber or fabric. Children can choose which side they wish for the underneath, but try to encourage them to use the 'non-slip' side if possible.

Use a felt pen for marking the shape of the soles and an ordinary pair of scissors for cutting them out. No special equipment is required.

Ask children to write their initials (or name) on each sole so that any mislaid can be returned to the right owner.

6. Paper bags

This work will, obviously, take more than one session to complete and it is a good idea to store each child's work in a separate paper bag, labelled with the appropriate name.

7. Garter stitch (plain knitting)

Knitting is the craft of looping wool so that it forms a fabric. In a way, it is a form of weaving, using two sticks. It is interesting to note that most left-handed people knit in the same way (direction) as right-handed people, although it may take them a little longer to acquire the knack.

Most people learn to knit in garter stitch as this is the most simple of the knitting stitches. In knitting patterns, garter stitch is denoted by the symbol K for knit.

How to begin the moccasins

(a) Double the wool and tie it in a loop.

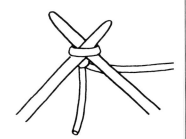

(b) Slide the loop on to the left-hand needle. Insert the right-hand needle at the back.

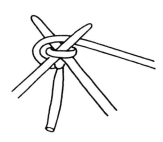

(c) Hold the short end of the wool in the left hand and wind the 'working' wool around the back of the right-hand needle and between.

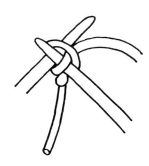

(d) Bring the right-hand needle through the loop together with the wool.

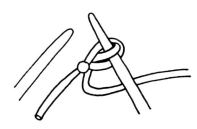

(e) Slide the stitch off the left-hand needle so that the new stitch appears on the right.

To increase

At the beginning or end of every row, it is necessary to make an extra stitch, as follows:

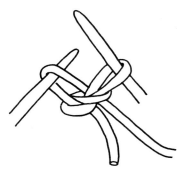

(a) Knit the first stitch but do not slide it off the left-hand needle.

(b) Insert the right-hand needle into the back of the old stitch.

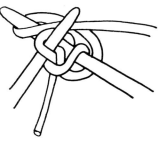

(c) Wind the 'working' wool around the back of the right-hand needle and between.

(d) Bring the right-hand needle through the loop, together with the wool.

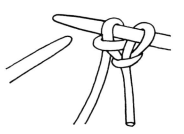

(e) Slide the new stitch off the left-hand needle so that it sits on the left of the old stitch.

Continue knitting normally on the remaining stitches.

Casting off

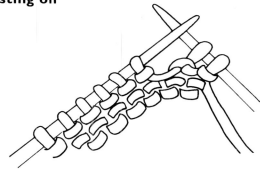

(a) Knit the first two stitches in the usual way.

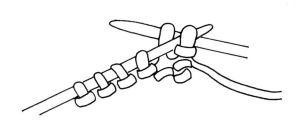

(b) With the left-hand needle, pick up the first stitch that you knitted.

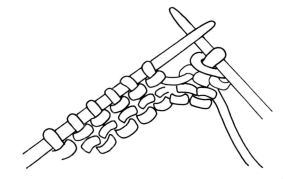

(c) Lift it over the second stitch and off the needle so that the loop is held in place. Continue knitting one stitch at a time and lifting the right-hand stitch over until only one stitch remains on the right-hand needle.

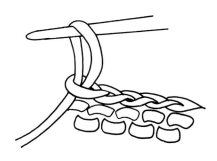

(d) Leaving a long end for sewing, cut the wool and pull it through the last stitch.

8. The Tie

Choose one of two methods to make the ties for the moccasins.

(a) Plaiting

Take three strands of wool measured to the length required and plait them as illustrated.

Move each outside strand to the centre, working alternately, left then right.

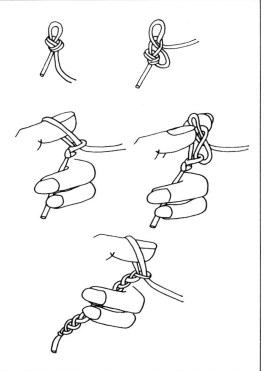

(b) Finger-knitting

Make a loop at one end of the ball of wool and thread more wool through the loop to make a second loop. Tighten this second loop over your thumb and pull more wool through to make a third loop. Insert your thumb again and tighten the chain by pulling the 'working' wool. Continue making loops over your thumb and tightening them up until the finger-knitting has grown to the length required. Cut the wool and pull it through the last loop to finish off. Thread the tie through the top of the moccasins and use the spare wool at each end of the tie to sew on the pom-poms.

9. Pom-poms

Chapter 6 gives detailed instructions on making half pom-poms. Use the same method for the pom-poms on these moccasins but make a full pom-pom by winding the wool round the complete circle, not just half-way. Again, any oddments of wool may be used for the pom-pom, no matter what the ply of the wool may be. This is a good way of using up some of the thinner wool which may have been considered too fine for the actual knitted part.

10. Patterned knitting

These moccasins can be worked in patterns other than ordinary garter stitch. Choose your own favourite knitting pattern and proceed in the same way as already described. However, other patterns may not produce such firm sides to the slippers as garter stitch does.

11. Embroidery

Give these moccasins an Eastern European look by knitting them in stocking stitch and embroidering the sides with coloured wools. Stocking stitch – one row knit and one row purl (which means inserting the right-hand needle into the *front* of each stitch so the knot appears on the same side of the work throughout) – is an ideal base for embroidery as each little 'V' shape can be counted as a square. The embroidery will also add body to the sides of the slippers because stocking stitch will make them feel rather flimsy.

Use cross-stitch for the decorative work, as shown in the following patterns or make up your own designs.

SUGGESTED PATTERNS FOR EMBROIDERY

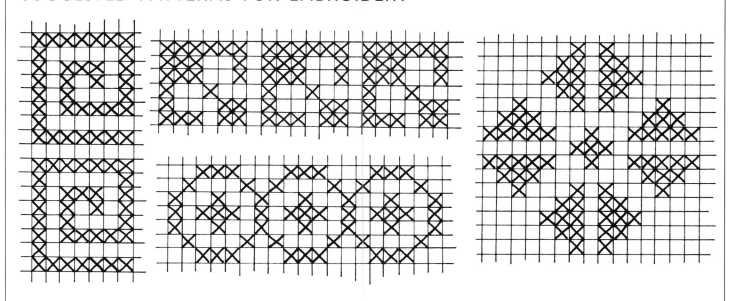

19 Bean Bag Toys

These simple-to-make bean bag toys are most appealing. Although they are not recommended for young children, the mouse especially may well find a home on mother's dressing-table.

METHOD (frog)

This is more straightforward than the mouse as there is only one pattern piece to sew. It is an easier pattern for children who are not experienced in handling a needle and thread as it will help them to learn the technique.

1. Trace the pattern piece for the frog which can be found at the end of this chapter.

2. Mark out the shape on felt – one dark green for the top and one light green for the underside.

3. Mark the position for the eyes, as shown on the pattern and attach these in the same way as for the mouse. (See p. 135).

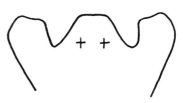

4. Pin the two bodies together and sew a line of small, neat running stitches from A, right round the frog's shape, to B, leaving the gap between its legs open. Sew back, from B to A, along the line already sewn, this time filling in the gaps. When finished, the sewing should look as though it has been done on a machine.

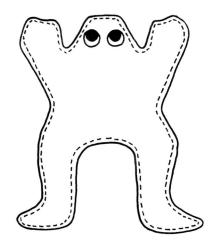

5. Fill the frog with the stuffing you have chosen – dried beans, rice or kapok.

6. Pin along the opening and sew, using the same method as before.

The frog can be decorated before it is sewn together, either by sewing coloured felt patches or other decorations on to its back, or even by sticking the decorative pieces in place.

METHOD (mouse)

1. Trace the pattern pieces for the mouse, which can be found at the end of this chapter.

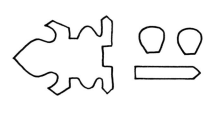

2. On a piece of white felt, mark and cut out 1 body, 2 ears and 1 tail.

3. On a piece of pink felt, mark and cut out 1 body, 2 ears and 1 tail.

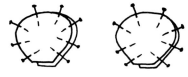

4. Pair the pieces together so that each white piece has a pink piece under it.

5. Pin the ears and tail in their pairs.

6. The ears
Sew a neat line of very small running stitches from A right round to B, leaving the bottom straight edge open. Then sew back, along the line already stitched, filling in the gaps. The finished work should look like a line of machine sewing.

7. The tail
Sew the white and pink tail pieces together in the same way as you did the ears, starting at A and working back again. Leave the straight end open.

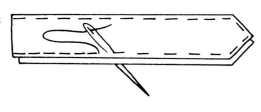

8. The face

Sew a neat line of small running stitches along the straight edge of one ear. Pull the stitches so that the felt is gathered slightly. Anchor the gathers by fastening off the thread. Sew the ear (pink side facing the front) on to the white head at the position marked on the pattern.

Sew the other ear to the head in a similar way.

Mark the position of the eyes, as shown on the pattern piece.

If using sew-on eyes, sew these into position.

If using the type of eyes which have a plastic stalk and fix through the fabric with a washer on the back, mark the position and cut a *very small* cross in the fabric into which each eye is to be inserted. Push the plastic stalk through the hole and push the washer on firmly to hold it in place.

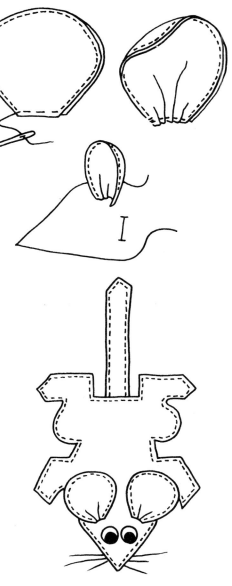

9. The body

Sew the two body pieces together using the same method of small running stitches which you used for the ears and tail. Leave the straight section between A and B open.

10. Fill the toy with the stuffing you have chosen – dried beans, rice or kapok.

11. Pin the tail in place (white side up) and sew across the straight edge, A to B, sewing as you have done before.

ORGANISING YOUR MATERIALS

1. Setting up the work area

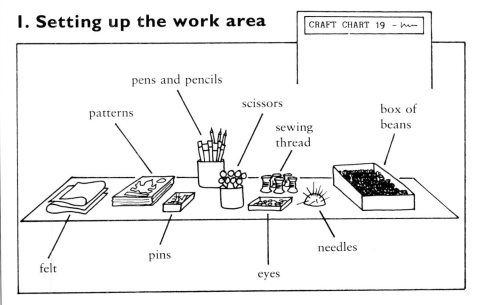

CRAFT CHART 19 –

pens and pencils

patterns

scissors

sewing thread

box of beans

felt

pins

eyes

needles

2. Patterns

Trace the patterns at the end of this chapter. Either photocopy enough patterns for each student to have a copy to cut out and pin to the felt or transfer your tracings to card and make sets of templates which the children can use to draw round on to the felt.

3. Felt

Felt is ideal for this type of toy but can be rather expensive for a large group. An alternative bonded material would be heavy weight vilene (white interfacing fabric used in dressmaking) which can be purchased by the metre from all fabric shops and department stores. Vilene is easily drawn on with a pencil and coloured with felt pens so that decoration can be added to the toy before sewing is started. Colouring in this way also gives individuality to the finished work, which might otherwise be quite plain and uninteresting.

If bonded fabric is not available, these toys can be made quite easily on the sewing machine. Allow a small turning on the edges of the pattern, sew round the pieces as instructed earlier but with right sides inside. The shapes can be clipped around the edges and turned so that the sewing is hidden inside. The opening, which has been left for the stuffing, can then be hand-sewn to complete the work.

4. Pins

Provide a box of ordinary dressmaking pins so that the felt shapes can be pinned together and held in place for sewing.

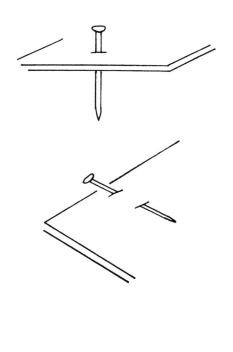

Pinning will be a new experience for many children, so don't be surprised to see pins just pushed straight through the pieces with the points sticking out at the other side.

Encourage the children to pin correctly by ensuring that the head and point of each pin are showing on the same side of the toy. Tell them to use an 'in-out' movement so that the pin goes through both thicknesses of fabric and comes back up again on the same side.

For safety, the points of the pins should be towards the centre of the work, their heads level with the edge of the shape. This prevents the pins from catching on other pieces of fabric and from sticking into fingers!

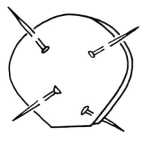

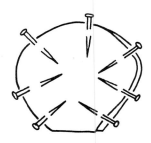

WRONG   RIGHT

5. Sewing thread

Provide the normal Sylko-type sewing thread in a selection of colours which will match the fabric available (white or pink for the mouse and green for the frog).

It is not necessary to provide a reel of cotton per child, or even per group. The thread can remain in a 'central pool' on the work surface and children can take a length at a time, as required.

6. Needles

A sewing needle (size 7) is recommended for hand-sewing. Refer to Chapter 15 for further suggestions on needles and an easy way for children to learn to thread them. It is surprising how much of a teacher's time is spent in threading needles for students.

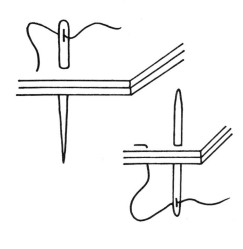

It is also suggested that each of the running stitches is approached in two separate movements – i.e. pushing the needle through both thickness of felt, downwards, bringing the thread right through, and then pushing the needle back up through both thicknesses of felt, to complete the stitch.

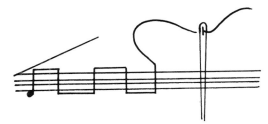

This ensures that the thread passes through the fabric at right-angles. It makes the stitches more equal in size and much easier to see on the return journey when filling in the spaces.

If one thinks about it, a stitch which is done all-in-one (i.e. in and out, as in normal sewing) means that the needle travels through the fabric at a steep angle and the stitch made at the back can often be very much smaller than the one seen on the top of the work.

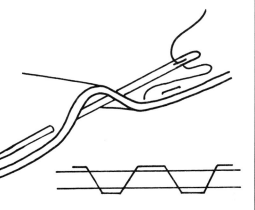

7. Eyes

Two types of eyes are suggested at the beginning of this chapter, the sort which has a shank and needs to be sewn on to the toy and the other which has a plastic stalk and is pushed through the fabric, to be held at the back with a grooved washer. Both types are easily obtainable from most fabric and accessory shops, craft shops or even market stalls. These days, eyes for toy-making come in a fabulous range of sizes, colours and designs. They are not expensive, just a few pence a pair, and most schools and leisure groups can arrange to purchase these from petty cash.

If children are intending to give the toy to a younger child, they should be aware of the safety of *all* the materials they use and it may be much safer to encourage them to cut small pieces of felt to make eyes and sew these on firmly, rather than use any types of eyes which may come off and be swallowed.

8. Stuffing

The name 'bean bag' toy implies that the toy should be filled with dried beans. But alternative fillings may be more suitable if the toy is destined for a younger child. Kapok is always available from fabric and craft shops, and a bag will fill quite a few toys.

If using dried beans or rice, make sure that the student has used small enough stitches around the shapes to prevent the stuffing from falling out between the stitches.

The advantage of using some form of dried pulse or rice, especially for the frog, is that the toy can be 'seated' in various positions and will hold that pose. Do note, however, that should a toy be left in the garden for any length of time the dried beans may start to grow and the toy will root to the ground!!

TEMPLATE FOR BEAN BAG TOY

A   B

MOUSE

A   B

A

B

TEMPLATE FOR BEAN BAG TOY

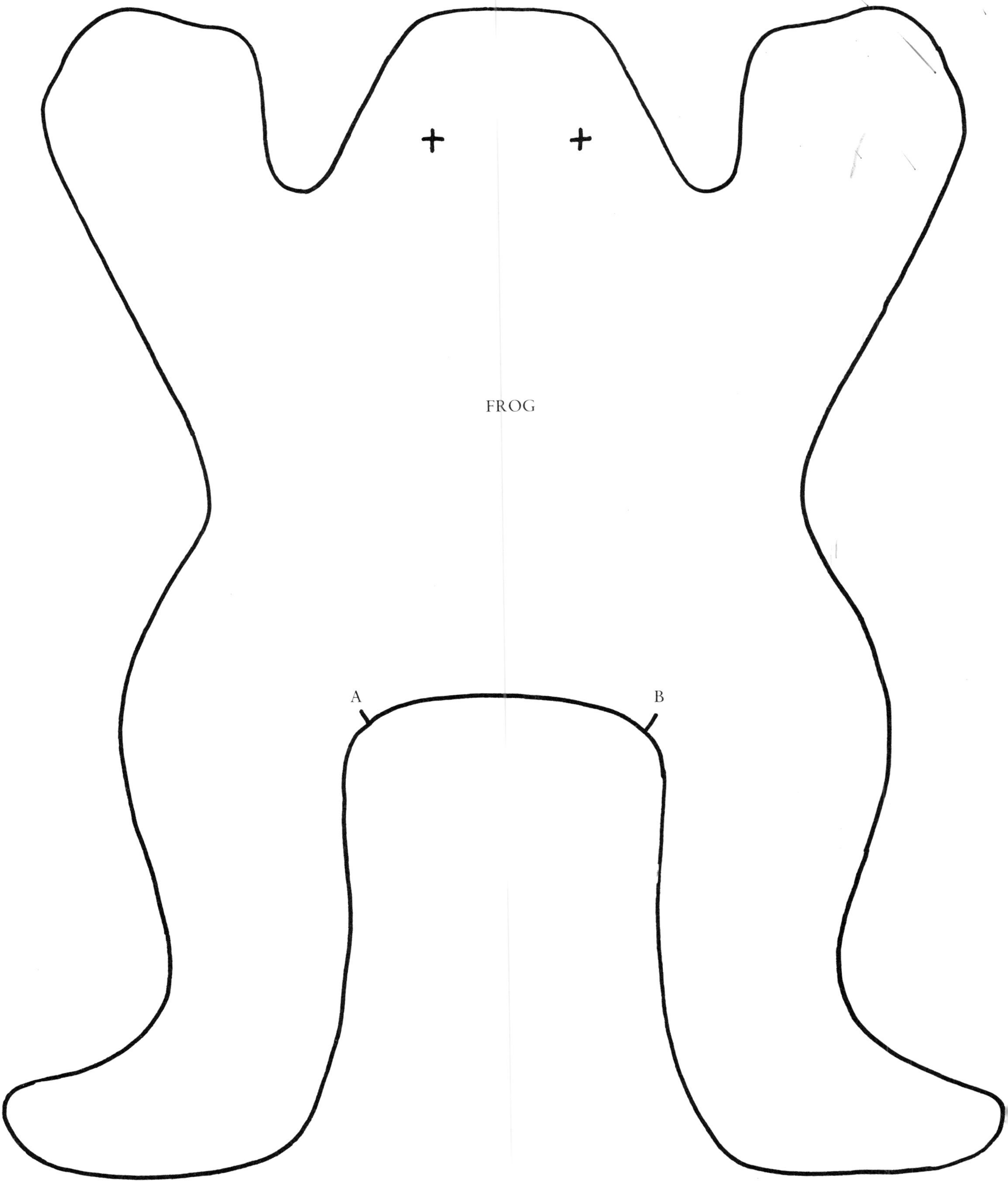

+   +

FROG

A   B

Appendix
CRAFT CHARTS

CRAFT CHART 0 — Stone Painting

① Choose a stone and draw a line right round it just over $\frac{1}{2}$ way down.

② Draw a design or picture on the top.

③ Paint each section of your design.

④ Go over the outlines with black paint. Leave to dry.

⑤ Cut out a circle of felt to fit the base.

⑥ Stick the felt to the base of the stone.

CRAFT CHART 2 – Finger Puppets

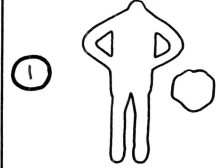

1. Take a template for a head and a body and draw round them on a piece of thick card.

2. Draw in all the details and colour. Outline in black.

3. Cut out the two shapes and stick the head to the body.

4. Bend the shoes forward so that they stand on the table.

GLUE

5. Make two tubes from thin card which fit your fingers.

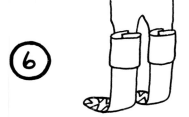

6. Stick the tubes to the backs of the puppet's legs.

CRAFT CHART 3 — Quilling

Roll the strip of coloured paper tightly round the cocktail stick.

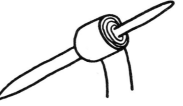

Practise making the following shapes:

① TIGHT ROLL
Slide the roll off the stick and glue the end in position to keep it tight.

② LOOSE ROLL
Pull the stick gently through the coil to open it. Glue as shown.

③ TEAR DROP
Open coil and glue as in ②. Gently pinch the top layers to a peak.

④ LEAF
Open coil and glue. Gently pinch both sides into peaks.

DOUBLE ROLL
Roll each end to the middle. Leave as tight coils or open and glue as shown.

⑥ SCROLL
Roll one end to centre - upwards. Roll other end to centre - downwards. Glue as required.

HEART
Fold strip in half. Roll ends inwards to centre. Glue as shown.

⑧ BEAK
Fold strip in half. Roll ends outwards to centre. Glue if required.

144

CRAFT CHART 4 – Paper Sculpture

1. Take a piece of card, draw round the pattern pieces and cut them out.

2. Roll head and body gently. Glue as marked.

3. Pull centre flaps of ears forward. Glue flaps to the inside of head.

4. Fit head into large end of body and glue where they touch. Keep body join up, head join down.

5. Mark nostrils on snout and glue to end of nose. Draw eyes.

6. Fold mane in half and fringe it. Open and glue centre line. Stick wide end on hog's forehead and the rest down the back join.

7. Roll and glue tusks either side of head, points upwards.

8. Roll leg pieces round a felt pen and glue to body.

9. Curl tail and stick inside body.

CRAFT CHART 5 – Silhouettes

Work with a partner

① Turn on the lamp and sit your partner on the chair.

② Fix a sheet of paper to the wall so that it catches the shadow of your partner's head and shoulders.

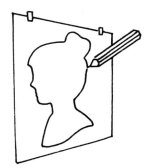

③ Draw round the shadow with a pencil.

④ Ask your partner to do the same for you.

⑤ Take your outline to the painting table and fill in the shape with paint.

Either:

⑥

Leave your silhouette on its background

Cut it out

Cut it out and mount it on coloured paper

CRAFT CHART 6 – Pom-pom Badges

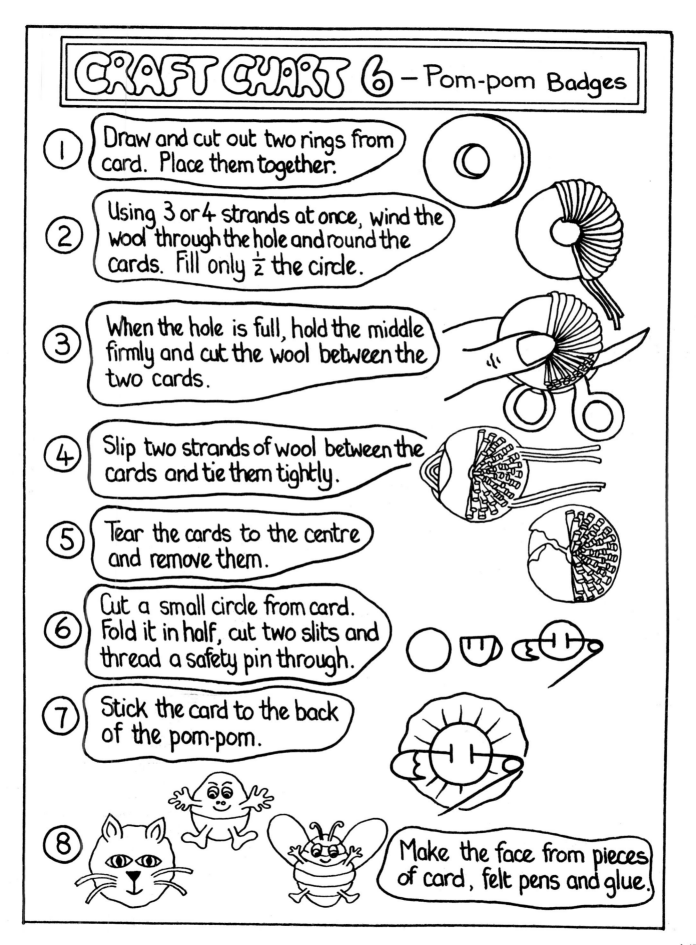

1. Draw and cut out two rings from card. Place them together.

2. Using 3 or 4 strands at once, wind the wool through the hole and round the cards. Fill only $\frac{1}{2}$ the circle.

3. When the hole is full, hold the middle firmly and cut the wool between the two cards.

4. Slip two strands of wool between the cards and tie them tightly.

5. Tear the cards to the centre and remove them.

6. Cut a small circle from card. Fold it in half, cut two slits and thread a safety pin through.

7. Stick the card to the back of the pom-pom.

8. Make the face from pieces of card, felt pens and glue.

CRAFT CHART 7 — Clay Owl Money Box

1. Take a piece of clay about the size of a tennis ball. Roll it into a smooth, round ball. Push your thumb into the centre.

2. Using your thumb inside and two fingers on the outside, press the clay evenly to hollow out the ball. DO NOT TOUCH THE RIM.

3. Make another pot in the same way.

4. Cradle the two halves in one hand, holding the rims together. Stroke the clay from the rims into the join so that no ridge shows.

5. Stand the hollow "egg" on the table and decorate it as an owl.

6. Mark a line at the back of the head for the money slot and a circle on the base to allow the money out. Work gently and smooth down all rough edges.

7. Make a clay disc for the base. Add clay to make the claws.

8. When both parts have dried, paint and varnish the owl.

CRAFT CHART 8 — Spiro-Lites

1. Colour two sets of planes A and B.

SET A   SET B

2. From set A, cut out one body, one big wing and one small wing. Glue them to card and cut them out.

3. Snip flaps on the body and fold up. Cut out remaining pieces and glue into place on the second side.

4. Glue wings to flaps. Make up the second plane in the same way.

5. Take a short piece of wire and bend it in to shape, evenly.

6. Use a paper clip to attach each plane to the ends of the wire.

7. Take a long wire. Wind it round a felt pen, to make a spring. Remove pen and pull spring open, gently, to form a spiral.

8. Fix one end of the spiral into a cork. Fit planes on spiral and cork the other end.

9. Planes should spin down the spiral. Turn wire upside-down for a return flight.

CRAFT CHART 9 - Masks

1) Draw round the templates of the basic mask and cut them out.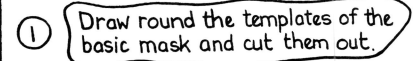

2) Fix the bands to the mask, as shown.

3) Hold the mask to your face, smooth the bands around and over your head.

4) Fix them together where they meet at the back.

Making the MONKEY MASK:

5) Draw round the templates for the monkey's face and ears. Cut them out.

6) Score along the dotted lines. Curve the eyebrows and glue the nostrils.

7) Fix the face to the basic mask (at point B). Glue tabs C, D, E and F to the basic mask - as shown.

8) Make up the ears - glue X over Y. Fix the ears to the monkey's head.

Try these too:

150

CRAFT CHART 10 – Papier Mâché Napkin Ring

① Tear up newspaper and white paper into 1cm squares. Keep them separated.

② Paste the inside of the ring.

③ Use the brush to pick up one piece of newspaper at a time and paste each one inside the ring.

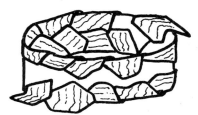

④ Continue all round the inside overlapping the pieces. They should stick out each side.

⑤ Paste the outside and fold the pieces over to make a neat edge – use your fingers.

⑥ Fill up all the gaps with newspaper pieces. Keep the edges neat.

⑦ Repeat stages ③ to ⑥ using white paper.

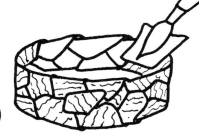

⑧ Paste one more layer of newspaper. Paste one more layer of white paper.

⑨ Paint the napkin ring with your own design.

⑩ When it is dry, varnish it.

CRAFT CHART 00 — Greetings Card Baubles

1. Cut out 20 circles from the greetings cards.

2. Place the triangle in the centre of each card disc and fold the three "wings" over.

3. Count them out into four groups of 5.

4. Lay out the first group into a flower shape and glue the "wings" together.

5. Make up the second group in the same way.

6. Glue the remaining discs around the bottoms of the two "caps"

7. Roll a piece of card and tie it tightly. Place the card inside the shape with the thread hanging out.

8. Slot the two halves together and glue the "wings" in place.

CRAFT CHART 12 – Space Game

1. Take a template of the rocket and engines. Draw round them on to card and cut them out.

2. Glue the body to silver foil. Glue the engines to coloured foil. Cut them out.

3. Glue the engines to the body as in the picture.

GLUE

4. Push a drawing pin through the centre of your rocket.

5. Write your name clearly on a piece of white card and colour the border.

Simon

6. Glue your name card to your rocket to cover the head of the drawing pin.

Simon

7. Pin your rocket to the game, ready to begin.

153

CRAFT CHART 13 — Collage

1. Cover a piece of card with material for the background.

2. Cut out the pattern pieces, number them and transfer them to coloured material.

3. Body – number 1: Glue in place on the background.

4. Head – number 2: Fix in position on body.

5. Stripes – numbers 3, 4, 5: Stick in place to make the bee's stripes.

6. Hands – numbers 6 and 7: Glue in place, as shown.

7. Legs – numbers 8 and 9: Add these to the picture.

8. Sting – number 10: Glue sting in place, pointing downwards.

9. Eyes – numbers 11, 12, 13, 14: Make up eyes and fix into position.

10. Wings – numbers 15, 16: Glue wings in place.

11. Outline all pieces with black wool.

CRAFT CHART 14 - Candlemaking

1. Remove a candle from the packet and trim it to the height of the kitchen funnel.

2. Break remaining candles into a clean baked bean tin and add a stub of coloured wax crayon. Stand tin in a saucepan of water on a stove, stirring occasionally.

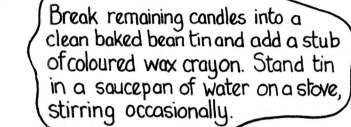

3. Stand funnel in a beaker of water which blocks the spout.

4. Hold white candle (wick down) in the funnel. Pour in a little wax to set candle in centrally.

5. Halve ice-cubes with a hammer and arrange them up the sides of the funnel.

6. Pour in coloured wax to fill funnel. Leave to set.

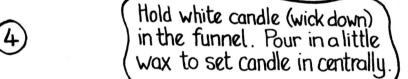

7. Unmould over a bowl.

CRAFT CHART 05 — Patchwork Tea Cosy

1. Use the templates to draw 14 hexagons, 12 half-hexagons and 8 ¾-hexagons on to card. Cut them out carefully.

   14 12 8

2. For each patch, cut material which is 2cm. bigger all round. Fold the edges over and sew, using tacking stitches.

3. Oversew the patches together.

4. Make up the two sides as shown.

5. Cut two pieces of thick blanket and sew them together, using back-stitch. Pin up the bottom to fit the cosy.

6. Remove the cards from the patchwork. Turn the cosy right side out and iron it.

7. Insert the blanket lining and sew around the bottom.

8. Anchor the blanket to the patchwork with small running stitches along the join.

9. Cover a curtain ring with coloured wool and sew it to the top of the teacosy.

CRAFT CHART 16 - Pop-up Puppet

① Make a hole in the yoghurt pot. Glue the rod into the cotton reel.

② Cut Santa's jacket from red, and his hands from pink material.

③ Glue the hands in place and join the jacket down one side.

④ Glue the pot at the bottom of the jacket and the cotton reel at the top.

⑤ Join up the other side.

⑥ Cover the pot and use black wool to make the bricks.

⑦ Cover the cotton reel in pink material.

⑧ Make up Santa's hat.

⑨ Cut his hair and whiskers from white material.

Add more details.

CRAFT CHART 17 — Découpage Piggy Bank

1. Remove the handle from the bottle and cut the money slit.

2. Tape card over the two holes.

3. Cut 2 wells from an egg box and tape them to make eyes. Cut 4 more to make the feet.

4. Cut two ears from card. Glue them to shape and tape them in place.

5. Tear newspaper into small squares and cover the bottle and top with a layer of papier mâché.

6. Repeat the papier mâché using white paper.

7. Make eyelashes from curled, black card.

8. Paint the eyes white and the rest of the pig in a bright colour.

9. Cut the decorations from card and paint the inserts.

10. Glue the decorations on to the pig and varnish him.

CRAFT CHART 18 - Knitted Moccasins

① Draw around your foot to make a paper pattern. Smooth round the outline.

② Draw round the pattern on to leatherette. Turn the shape over for the other foot.

③ Starting with one stitch, increase at the beginning or end of every row until there are 20 stitches. Knit a strip long enough to go round your foot.

④ Cast off. Make another strip to match.

⑤ Sew the ends together to join the strips into rings.

⑥ Pierce holes evenly around the edges of the two soles.

⑦ Oversew the knitting to the soles.

⑧ Make a tie for each moccasin and pom-poms for the ends of the ties.

CRAFT CHART 19 - Bean Bag Toys

① Cut out the mouse patterns in white felt.

② Cut out the mouse patterns in pink felt.

③ Pin the pieces together in their pairs.

④ Sew the ears and tail. Use small running stitches from A round to B.

⑤ Sew back along the line of stitches, filling in the gaps.

⑥ Gather the ears and sew them to the head.

⑦ Sew or fix the eyes in place.

⑧ Sew the two body pieces together from A round to B and back again to fill in the gaps.

⑨ Pour the beans into the body.

⑩ Put the tail in place and sew up the opening.